S0-BQT-741

Betty, Blue Belle and Bitch

Betty Krawczyk

Copyright © 2013 by Betty Krawczyk
First Edition – October 2013

Published by Schiver Rhodes Publishing

ISBN
978-1-4602-2628-5 (Hardcover)
978-1-4602-2629-2 (Paperback)
978-1-4602-2630-8 (eBook)

All rights reserved.

No part of this publication may be reproduced in any form, or by any means, electronic or mechanical, including photocopying, recording, or any information browsing, storage, or retrieval system, without permission in writing from the publisher.

Produced by:

FriesenPress
Suite 300 – 852 Fort Street
Victoria, BC, Canada V8W 1H8

www.friesenpress.com

Distributed to the trade by The Ingram Book Company

I would like to acknowledge with thanks the excellent work and expertise of my editor, Darby Carswell, who went above and beyond the call of duty in the process of getting this book together. I would also like to thank the staff at FriesenPress for making the printing process as stress free as humanly possible.

Front cover: sculptures and photos from
the legacy of Joseph Albert Cuchiara, Jr.

Back cover: photo of Harriet Nahanee under arrest
at Eagleridge Bluffs, courtesy of North Shore News

Back cover: author's photo courtesy of Susan Robertshaw

Inside photo: dedication page photo of
Harriet Nahanee courtesy of Rob Baxter

This book is dedicated to the memory of Harriet Nahanee (Dec. 7, 1935-Feb. 24, 2007) who died shortly after her release from prison where she was incarcerated for defending the ancestral lands of her children and grandchildren. I believe Harriet Nahanee's spirit still occupies the destruction site at Eagleridge Bluffs, that the prayers and songs she offered for the dead and dying creatures there are still whispered in the rocks and crevices of the site. I believe Harriet Nahanee's spirit lives among her people and in and with those of us who joined hands with her to demand loving care for this earth and for each other. And for all our relations.

Table of Contents

CHAPTER ONE
My Inner House

IT IS THE MONTH OF JANUARY, 2009. OVER A YEAR SINCE I
was released from prison in the aftermath of the Eagleridge Bluffs wars and
Harriet Nahanee's premature death. The native Squamish elder fell in the
trenches during the struggle, so to speak, and this new manuscript I am
writing will probably never get out of the neighbourhood. But I don't care;
I haven't been writing for a general audience since when anyway.

Lately I write mostly for a crazy little ole lady who lives inside my head.
I am eighty years old but I think this crazy lady is even older. And she has
been bothering me since I have known her. For many years I have banished
her to back rooms with no sunlight and starvation diets, hoping she will
die. The old bitch hasn't - in fact, she is getting stronger and seems determined to last as long as I do. But my feelings toward her have recently
changed. Because of Ray Allen, my brother, who died a few months back.
Except for me, Ray Allen was the last of my generation of siblings and first
cousins, people who all knew each other as children. I am the last man
standing. Or woman.

I'm next. And I can see my own mortality slinking around the corner
of my inner house like a chicken-eating hound dog. I know when I die
this crazy ole lady will die too, and she's demanding her fifteen minutes
to tell what she knows, or thinks she knows. I owe her that. Without her
help I would never have survived those bizarre years in prisons - over three
years all told. Nor for that matter, some of the even more bizarre situations
that arose over the years from trying to raise eight children and four husbands. The children were a snap compared to the husbands. Frequently the

children were fun and funny; the husbands rarely were. It was the times, my daughters tell me. Way back then when I was marrying and divorcing, men were more sexist. Times have changed, they insist. So I have decided to draw back the curtains and inspect the little ole lady's crazed condition with an open mind. In fact, we have been visiting so frequently lately that I'm feeling quite chummy with her and have taken to calling her Bitch instead of Witch, the name I used to call her.

Anyway, Witch doesn't exactly describe this old woman who lives in one of the compartments of my inner house. Bitch more accurately describes my old friend. She thinks we may be approaching the end times, not because of Biblical prophecy, which she sneers at, but because women haven't had the guts so far to try to stop it.

Bitch is enough to frighten children on sight. She would be equally at home at a Halloween party or cruising the streets of Vancouver's downtown Eastside. Her tall, gaunt frame and multi-coloured hair are bad enough, but coupled with the baggy tops and long skirts she favours, she is grotesque. Gothic grunge. Ridiculous get-up for a woman her age. Lately Bitch has taken to wearing tight blue jeans under the baggy tops. The jeans are fashionably torn at one knee. I have complained about her lack of fashion sense but she pretends not to hear. Like my daughter's cat Hoffman, when I am fussing at her (Hoffman is a she) Bitch gives me a cold stare, sniffs, and stalks off.

But I can't dismiss either one with disdain. They both know me, and they both know I feel responsible for them. Hoffman isn't my equal as far as intellect goes but I have to struggle to stay ahead of Bitch's constant intellectual challenges.

At first glance you might dismiss Bitch as an elderly hippie woman who had been doing the drop out, turn on thing way too long. But no, when you look into her crinkled face and the dark eyes in their deep sockets, you know there is something else there. Something fiercely independent and keenly intelligent. Something that dispels the notion of senility or insanity. Sometimes her gaze freaks me out and I have to drop my eyes and turn away. It's as though she sees through me, that her steady gaze is like a challenge of some sort that must be met. And I don't call her Bitch to her face although she would probably laugh.

I am actually working with her quite nicely when the doorbell rings. We have been working on the "Grandmother Hypothesis." Bitch disappears at the sound of the doorbell. I get up from the computer with some annoyance and walk to the door. I hate the peek-a-boo little thing in the apartment door that distorts even dearest familiar family members into images of escaped mass murderers. The present vision of a fair-haired young woman looking eagerly into the bowels of the door has a hideously bloated face.

"Who is it?" I ask, trying to remember if I have some kind of appointment this morning. I have a love-hate relationship with my appointment book. I write in it, lose it under a pile of papers, find it, and lose it again.

"It's Toby Matthews, Mrs. Krawczyk. From the Women Wranglers Forum. I was to come at ten this morning."

Oh, right. The young woman from some kind of a women's project. She called last week. She wanted a few words from me for their radical women's publication. I open the door. Without the peek-hole glass distortion I see Toby Matthews has quite a normal young woman face. She is pleasantly pink-cheeked, from health and vitality or makeup, I can't tell, women's makeup is so clever these days. At eighty I am not expected to use makeup but I do anyway when I go out, or for company. Just a bit. Just a tad of colour, you know. And my God, my eyebrows are as white as my hair. Without a little eyebrow pencil it's as though I have no eyebrows. So I usually dib and dab here and there, trying to create a bit of definition in a face that just wants to give up and slide into an undifferentiated blob of comfortably sagging flesh. It's kind of like trying to keep a pan of too-hastily prepared biscuits from sliding into each other in the baking pan and becoming one big soggy hoe cake instead of the crisp, separate biscuits that are so tasty. But that's okay. That's what old faces and too-hastily prepared biscuit dough are supposed to do. And while I may be caught unaware at the moment I am decently dressed and except for my work area, the apartment looks almost presentable. Often, neither of these things happens. At least not at the same time. Often I have trouble even finding my desk for the mound of papers and books that seem to rise by levitation from the carpeted floor.

I bid my young visitor come in and sit, offer coffee or tea. She accepts tea and after a bit of fussing with the teapot we are comfortably seated, she on the sofa, I across from her in my old office chair. Her smile is bright and forthright.

"Mrs. Krawczyk..." she begins, and then pauses.

"My last name is actually Schiver," I say, more to help her out than anything. That's what southern women are taught to do. Don't let conversational pauses last too long. The men might start fighting if you do. It becomes second nature to women to keep conversation flowing regardless of the situation. "That's my maiden name," I go on. "I'm thinking about taking it back. Before I die. But in my own culture..." And then I pause. Suddenly I feel stupid talking about my own culture. Women don't have a distinct, recognizable culture. Not in a patriarchal world. At least that's what I'm told by Bitch. And she has convinced me.

"Yes?" the young woman asks, gently encouraging me. A tape recorder has appeared on her lap on top of a sheaf of papers. She sees me looking at it.

"Oh, if you don't want this recorded, I can put it away; it was just that when I asked you on the phone you said it was okay..."

Oh, what the hell. Whatever, as the kids say.

"It's okay," I answer.

"You were saying that in your culture..."

"Yes," I respond, snapping out of a momentary lapse. The lapses have nothing to do with old age. All my children and husbands have complained at various times in our relationships that I often seem to go away to other climes in the midst of conversation. The girls have been teasing me ever since they first heard about Alzheimer's, saying that if I ever got it, how would they even know?

"Yes, Louisiana culture, that is," I go on. "I would at this point tell you that you could call me Miss Betty, as I am an elder. But you can do that anyway, and I'll call you by your first name, too. It's Toby isn't it?"

"Yes, ma'am. It's Toby. But in Louisiana senior women are called Miss?"

I like her use of the phrase "senior women." Her question implies that she doesn't understand why elder women are called "Miss" down south. I don't really know myself, except that it is both a mark of familiarity and a mark of respect. But one has to have permission to use this title with an older woman and it is always used in conjunction with a woman's first name. And this is true of elderly black women as well as white. If an older woman is addressed by her last name by someone she doesn't know well that's okay, but if he or she uses Miss with her first name, it's a social blunder. This holds true regardless of whether the woman is married or has ever been married. At least that's the way it used to be; no telling what is going on down there now. I haven't stepped foot in Louisiana mud since my mother died. She died on my seventieth birthday.

"Okay, Toby, now tell me. What is it you want from me? I've already written and talked a lot about the forests of BC and how they're being destroyed and all about my prison sentences…"

"I know. I've researched your activism record. This is somewhat different. We're looking at gender and social relations. The research I'm doing is about a question, specifically, a question that men seem to be forever asking and that is…what do women really want? Women in general give so many diverse answers to this question I thought I might come ask what you thought about what it is women want. Would you care to comment on this question?"

I stare at her for a moment, trying to make sense of her question. She gives a nervous little smile. "On the question of what it is women really want," she repeats.

I sit my tea cup down on the rickety little side table by my chair. I plan to ditch the table when I move. Which I hope is soon.

"You're not talking about a sex thing, are you?" I ask uncertainly. "You wouldn't be asking an 80 year old woman that kind of question?"

A rosy blush quickly spreads over her fair features. Her round grey eyes express horror at the very idea.

"No, ma'am, I don't mean it in that context…well, it might be in that context for some women, but in broader, more general terms, why is it that men are always baffled, or pretend to be baffled, by what women want and I thought that being an elder you might be able to throw some light on this, you know, in general, because you've been married, what? Four times? I don't mean to be disrespectful, but you write these things yourself and you talk about the relationship between men and women…"

I nod. "So you think I'm some kind of expert on what women want?

She shuffles her papers. "Well, no ma'am, it's just that nobody ever asks older women, you know, really older women, like I don't mean you're that old, but…"

I wait for her to clarify her thoughts. She rises to the occasion and takes a deep breath.

"I just thought it was time for somebody to ask some women around your age the same question we're asking younger women. I think it's past time, really."

I laugh. "My God, Toby, you're a pioneer," I say, warming to the interview.

"How old are you?"

"Twenty-four."

"Well, I certainly agree that if you want to ask about marriage then it's probably a good idea to ask somebody who has had experience. Why not? Why ask somebody who has only done it once, whatever the question under consideration? Except dying, of course. Let's see. You want a specific answer right now to the question...What is it that women want, or wanted in my day and how does that square with what I think they might want now?"

Toby leans back on the sofa and smiles.

"Exactly," she says.

I pause again: a mistake. It's just time enough for Bitch to part the curtains between my real world and hers and start in with her rasping stage whispers. She's becoming impossibly aggressive. Not at all like the prim little lady who lives in the front compartment of my inner house. That little lady has a big sunshiny front window in her apartment and usually waits to be invited before commenting on anything. However, Blue Belle, as I call this other creature I live with, has become somewhat more aggressive herself. I call her Blue Belle because she usually wears a little blue organdy dress with puffy sleeves and a flared skirt. Blue Belle is the opposite of Bitch in every way. She is young and prissily pretty with blonde curly hair.

"To rule the world," I say, mouthing out loud the words that Bitch is busily inserting into my brain. I am passively accepting Bitch's dictation. After all, I am keeping my promise to her. To give her the stage for a bit. "That is what women want because they know it is the only way women and children will be free of the fear of men," I say firmly.

"Really!" my visiting reporter gasps, her expressive eyes again registering something akin to horror. And then she smiles uncertainly. "To rule the world? Do you think women really want to rule the world?"

"They may not recognize it as such," I respond dutifully, prodded by Bitch. "But they will have to eventually because male rule is killing everything: the earth, people on it, fish, animals, the entire earth experience, in fact. It's all going. Women have to make up their minds to either take over the whole kit and caboodle or passively accept extinction of everything, including themselves. And their children, of course."

"And men," Toby adds.

"Yes. Although men have already got a head start on liquidating themselves. Do you know the chemicalization of industry is not only linked to a fifty per cent drop in male sperm count but also to the feminization of the sperm count? That the very composition of the chromosomes in sperm is changing?"

No, Toby hasn't heard any of this. So that by the time she leaves an hour later, Bitch is exhausted from explanations and willingly retreats to the cool darkness of the back room where she lives out her somewhat learned but miserable life. I am exhausted, too. I head for the couch, then pause for a moment to peek in on Blue Belle. I hope she hasn't been too traumatized by the interview. But my hopes are dashed. Blue Belle is sitting on her blue chaise lounge by the big picture window, holding her head in her hands, sobbing into what had been a freshly ironed hankie a few minutes before.

Blue Belle has an amazing stack of dainty little hankies. Some of them have embroidered tiny pink roses or blue bells in the corners, some are finished with homemade lace like my mother used to make. I mentally gird my loins for battle, so to speak.

"What?" I demand. "What is so terrible?"

Blue Belle raises her curly blonde head and looks at me with red, accusing eyes. There is a long moment's silence. And then I have to wait until she finishes blowing her perky little nose until it's as red as her eyeballs.

"You know what," she says finally, her voice still sobby and hiccuppy. "You know very well what. You let that old witch say those terrible things about marriage and about...God..."

"Well, that wasn't all she said," I answer defensively. "She said some good things, too, things that even you would agree with...like how children aren't being protected..."

Blue Belle's reddened blue eyes flash.

"She wants to get rid of men!" she shrieks. "Don't you understand? She wants to get rid of men!"

"That isn't true," I protest. "That isn't really what she's saying…"

Blue Belle jumps to her feet and shakes two little clenched fists at me. "Yes it is, yes it is, yes it is…and she's going to ruin all the hard work you've done for the environment! Not only that…I think…I think she wants to kill you!"

It's no use. I can't talk to her when she's like this. I close the door on her and look for my airplane pillow in the basket behind the couch. I don't fly, at least when I can help it, but I do like airplane pillows. I find the pillow and try to settle down for my mid-day nap. I am blessed with the ability to sleep soundly under the most adverse conditions and that includes naps, but still, Blue Belle's ringing accusations bug me. I can't settle into the couch as usual. My body memory among the couch cushions is elusive. I turn several different ways, restless and troubled. I know Bitch doesn't really want to kill me; after all, I am her mouthpiece.

But Bitch is after Blue Belle. The two have been at each other's throats since they became aware of each other many years ago. I've put up with their yapping at me and at each other forever because they have nowhere else to go. But they wear me out. They cannot make peace. Blue Belle is a fundamentalist Bible thumper. Which is somewhat unusual as her grand-parents on her father's side were Jewish immigrants from somewhere in northern Germany who came to America in the 1800's and wound up, for whatever reason, in Louisiana. They accepted Jesus as a passport to physical safety in a violent rural southern culture that had a thing about Jews as well as Blacks. It helped that Blue Belle's ancestors were blond and blue-eyed, and didn't look like foreigners.

Bitch, the back room occupant in my inner house, is Cajun. She's all mixed up with French and Indian and God only knows what else. Unlike Blue Belle, Bitch goes anywhere her mind takes her. She scares me at times, which is why I have tried to keep a tight rein on her in the past. Blue Belle never scares me, she just annoys me, but I can't disown her. She, too, has rights. But Blue Belle and Bitch are too different to make peace and often I would just like to declare a pox on both their houses, and their respective rooms in my inner house, and toss them both out. But I can't. They're part of me. And they make me think. Besides, they're both zealots which can be entertaining at times unless I'm very tired. Which I am at the moment. My brain gradually begins to fuzz with mid-day nap syndrome and I sleep.

I'm a dream junkie. I love dreams, mine and everybody else's. There is no way to adequately describe a dreamscape in a written context as dreams are non-verbal, but when I wake from the couch I am stuffed with them... and these dreams were all about houses. It's because my daughter Marian is looking for a house, one big enough for the two of us and my grandson Rhodes. Rhodes is eighteen. He is the son my daughter Barbara Ellen left behind when she died of breast cancer. Rhodes was only four years old at the time.

A month after my interview with Toby from the Women Wrangler's Forum, Marian and I, along with her boyfriend Justin, are on our way to inspect the house of our dreams. To avoid confusion I might mention that Marian, Rhodes, Justin, and Hoffman the cat, are not just psychic squatters within my inner landscape, they are real. Very real.

So are the disgusting things happening in Vancouver at the moment. In the whole province for that matter. I just want out of the city. As long as I'm in the midst of the swirl of super-charged energy in Vancouver I can't think. Nobody can actually think very coherently in such a mess, with the true cost of the Olympics rising to numbers incomprehensible to most of us and the drug kids (I call them kids because that's mostly what they are; young boys faced with the choice of working for MacDonald's for six dollars an hour or pushing drugs for a couple of thousand a week choose the latter) are killing each other way too frequently over turf, while increasing numbers of people are joining the ranks of the unemployed. Not to mention the poor babies already in the street. The ones hopelessly addicted.

Yes, poor babies, because that's what they are, emotionally at least, babies who didn't get what they needed from anybody as babies and remain forever emotionally impaired. The needle is the breast of sweet mother love. Why deny them? Give them what they so desperately crave and let's take care of them. That's the only decent thing to do. Legalize all drugs. Declare addiction a health problem. Let the medical profession, many of whom are addicted themselves to both legal and non-legal drugs, take care of the situation. They know what to do.

So the break from the city is welcome as Marian and I, along with Justin, begin our house hunt on the east side of Vancouver Island on February 14, Valentine's Day of 2009.

Marian, an independent researcher, can work almost anywhere, at least part of the time, and is also trying to do a PhD in Medical Anthropology. But I don't know about this little town we're heading into as a possibility for a change of life style. The town lies in a mid-range valley. There is snow on the ground. And the town is, well, little. However, there are larger towns relatively near; we wouldn't be isolated. But Blue Belle, dainty Southern flower that she is, is awake and on duty. She likes the purity of the air but is desperately trying to bring my attention to the amount of snow on the ground. Snow just lying around on the ground panics her. Louisiana doesn't have snow and Blue Belle isn't crazy about anything foreign. She likes air conditioning and iced teas and melons and sherbets but no ice or snow around her house, thank you. Or what she perceives as her house. But it's not even that cold, for Pete's sake, so I ignore her.

Bitch is sleeping. She doesn't care where we go. Creature comforts are immaterial to her. The third house we look at is a winner. I love it. And evidently, from her expressions of barely concealed delight, Marian does, too. It is an old character house, upgraded, with lots of room for all our relatives to visit and Justin, too, and his children from a previous marriage along with a big workshop for Rhodes. Huge yard. Greenhouse. An enormous cedar tree and an equally enormous cherry tree. Even a large wisteria vine on the back deck.

Perfect. Back at our bed and breakfast Marian calls her older sister Rose Mary. Rose Mary, her husband and two daughters live on the west coast of the Island. We tell them about the house. Rose Mary is uneasy about the price and our ability to pay even with everyone pitching in. But it doesn't matter because we find out later that although we have been shown the house there's already an accepted offer on it. Back to the city, discouraged. Our dream house, snatched from under our noses.

I handle disappointment and rejection well. And grief. After all, I have experienced so much of it, the loss of a sweet ole house with a cherry tree and a cedar tree is just a minor annoyance. The death of Barbara Ellen, Rhodes' mother, fourteen years ago, threatened at the time to seriously derail me. Then five years ago when Joey, my eldest, died from brain cancer, my world again began to crumble at the outer edges of my sanity and emotional balance. But with the help of my other children and grandchildren, and time, blessed time, the dark folds smothering my life began gradually to lift. And Rhodes needed me. Life, as long as there is breath, goes on. But these past two months have been particularly hard.

I ran for mayor of Vancouver in the last municipal election under the auspices of the Work Less Party. Work Less, Live more, Love more. That was our slogan. But the working less part began to take on an ironic twist even during the election. How to convince somebody who has no job that working less is a good thing? That sharing work enables people to have more time for family, community, politics, even art? I didn't get many votes as Gregor mania was going on (Gregor Robertson being a young, good-looking politician who made his fortune, so to speak, on rather pricey organic juice drinks served up in plastic bottles with a happy name, and rode into office via more than a few corporate supporters). Who would vote for an 80 year old jailbird great-grandmother anyway? And Gregor Robertson seems to be taking hold of the job in a reasonable fashion despite all the baggage he carried in with him.

However, the studious way in which the newspapers and even the local CBC ignored my run for mayor made me wonder. After all, I was fairly well known in Vancouver as an environmental activist. Just on the strength of my having spent over three and a half years in BC prisons fighting logging companies, my run might have added a little colour. I had also been included in several films, articles, books and environmental studies programs, besides being a writer myself. And consider...I had the dubious distinction of being the only person convicted of anything whose supporters shut down the entire Supreme Court building in Vancouver in protest for most of the afternoon when I was sentenced. Yes, by all accounts I should have been included with at least a sentence or two in the local media line up of candidates. But nada.

I couldn't believe it. Then to make matters worse, Conrad Schmidt, the founder of the Workless Party, who had recruited me from prison to run as mayor under the Workless Party banner and who was also acting as my campaign manager, jumped ship in the middle of the campaign and joined Gregor Robertson's Vision campaign. I was stunned. I had never heard of such a thing. This was worse than Louisiana politics. Not that I expected to be elected or even come close. That would have been silly. But I did want to make a decent showing so that people would listen to what I had experienced in the forests of British Columbia.

Directly following this disappointing political venture my brother Ray Allen died after a protracted illness. He died in Arizona where he lived in the high desert with his wife and youngest son.

I got sick shortly after. I'm rarely sick. A really vicious bug moved into my body's flora and fauna. To compound matters, there was a book fiasco. A terrible printing error in my latest book; Open Living Confidential: From Inside the Joint. My first two books ~ Clayoquot: the Sound of my Heart, and Lock Me Up or Let Me Go: The Protests, Arrest and Trial of an Environmental Activist and Grandmother ~ had been issued by Canadian publishers but the third book was my first try at self-publishing and whole pages were missing. I had to recall books already sold and given away and send out new copies.

And then I was kicked out of court. Again. This was a civil suit I had brought against Kiewit Sons Co. and one of their employees, and also included Kevin Falcon, Minister of Transportation, the Ministry of Transportation and Sea to Sky Investment. I claimed that I was assaulted within the legal definition of assault on my last blockade at Eagleridge Bluffs by a Kiewit Sons employee. Mr. Justice Cullen ruled that I wasn't assaulted because at any time I could have moved away from the huge rock truck I claimed was deliberately backing into me. Even if I was in danger (which I was and had the film to prove it), the judge said I could have moved out of the way at any time.

This kind of judgment is typical of my dealings with the Supreme Court in British Columbia. In spite of the history of peaceful civil disobedience around the world, in spite of the fact that almost all the rights and freedoms that we enjoy in this country and the US were put there by somebody's civil disobedience, the judges here act like they've never heard of it; certainly they don't understand it. If Mr. Justice Cullen understood anything about civil disobedience he would know that the purpose of a blockade is not to move away in the face of threatening machinery. If one moves when one is being threatened, the blockade is over. I could not move away: it was impossible within the context of peaceful civil disobedience. And I had the right to make a protest even though I knew I would probably go to prison for it and the driver of the truck in question did not have the right to physically threaten me.

However, as long as judges like Mr. Justice Cullen believe that I (or any of the other protesters) don't actually have the right to practice peaceful civil disobedience, then some workers, when they get a chance, will play chicken with me (us) using their big ole trucks and machinery. It's a very dangerous game. And the men who do this should be punished. Instead they are protected by the BC courts.

I was part of a protest in 2000 where an estimated one hundred loggers employed by Interfor (International Forest Products) attacked eight young people who were camping in the Elaho Valley just north of Vancouver. The young people were just observing the rate of clear cutting; they weren't trying to stop it. But the loggers felt threatened by any outside observation and one morning, by appointment, met, marched to where the young observers were camping and fell upon them with a vengeance. The loggers destroyed the young people's cameras and burned their tents and belongings. They also beat the observers physically, sending three to hospital, including a woman.

The judge in this case sentenced the bully loggers ~ who had committed illegal physical assault resulting in bodily harm to young people who had a right to be in public woods ~ to anger management courses. That's what they got. And what did we protesters (I was so upset about the way the young people were treated I went to the Elaho myself and continued the blockade) receive?

Two of us got the stiffest prison sentences ever handed out for protesting. Mr. Justice Parrott sentenced me and Barney Kerns each to a year in prison with no hope of parole, the equivalent to a three-year sentence with parole. Even though we appealed after six months and won, I am still smarting about such a rank miscarriage of justice. And this personal feeling of injustice was compounded by the Eagleridge Bluffs struggle which I believe drastically hastened Harriet Nahanee's death because of a totally bizarre incarceration ordered by Madam Justice Brown of the Supreme Court of BC.

So I had welcomed Marian's suggestion that we should both get out of the city for a period of recuperation. We returned to the city disheartened at having our dream house snatched away from us. But all was not lost: the following Thursday we received a phone call from the realtor. The accepted offer on our dream house on the Island house had fallen through. Marian could now make an offer of her own.

Ah, escape. A place where I could write in peace. Where Marian could exercise her right to home ownership in a little country town. Where Rhodes could perhaps start his own electronic repair business, computer geek that he is. Or go to college. A place big enough for all and sundry to share country air and good fellowship. But no. Snakes appeared in the garden. Not little garden snakes, but deadly boa constrictors. The bloody house is a hundred and fifteen years old and the entire thing needed rewiring and unless it got it nobody could get insurance. At this news Blue Belle sat back with a smug smirk on her face. She doesn't want to go anywhere where snow doesn't just immediately melt like it does in Vancouver anyway. For her, Vancouver was the limit.

However, it is now several weeks later and we are back on track in pursuit of the house. The seller is doing the required rewiring. The inspector who will say yea or nay to the question of fire insurance will appear next Saturday. Six more days and we will know. I have become quite enthusiastic about this house. It is old, like me, but has a spacious forgiving heart.

I will occupy the master bedroom on the south east side that has a small deck. I can just step out on my private deck every morning and have early coffee in the sunrise. And sunshine had better come with this house. Lots of it. I haven't had early coffee on my own deck since I left the south. God, what a luxury! If the house falls through now I think I'll cry. So will Blue Belle; even though she doesn't like snow she has reconciled herself. She says the house has begun to remind her of old southern country houses, smaller of course, and not as grand, but substantial enough.

At the other end of my inner house Bitch says she doesn't give a continental damn where we live but she does dread the confusion of moving. She can't think when things get too confused. But she is pleased that I have been invited to a university student forum on prostitution back in the city. The forum is several days away and she is already trying to program into my brain the points that I should emphasize. There is nothing that so maddens her as the fact of prostitution.

CHAPTER TWO
City Blues

BARACK OBAMA HAS JUST LEFT THE BUILDING. HE WAS with us Canadians for several hours yesterday. I like the man. So does everybody. But in spite of all the wishing here and around the world, Obama is not Jesus Christ and this is not the second coming even though some of the Muslims are starting to claim him, too. And yes, suddenly...oh, suddenly! There is this acceptance of Sharia law in Pakistan in the areas where the Taliban roam. Sharia law. Did Obama have anything to do with encouraging this? Just about the only good excuse the US and UN have for staying the course in Afghanistan (which involves Pakistan) is to help the women of these countries come out from under the veil. And now there is this sudden acceptance of Sharia law along the Pakistan borders under control of the Taliban. Good grief! This turn of events awakens Bitch. I leave the breakfast table and turn off the radio.

"See, I told you," Bitch admonishes. "Christians and Muslims are indeed brothers. They have this one fundamental absolute in common. That woman must be kept captive."

"Oh, get out," I answer crossly. It is Sunday and Marian's offer on the house in Merryland has not been accepted. "Marian and I are not captive. We are trying to establish a household."

"And you will encounter much resistance."

"Things have changed," I snap. "The person we were trying to buy the house from is a woman. A professional woman. Is she a captive, too?"

"Of course. She's a professional. That means she's a female version of a man because all professions under patriarchy express male thinking. To become a professional anything, even a whore, women have to learn to think like men. Female culture is so long gone women can't even remember having it. We used to have our own separate language, too. Did you know that?"

Oh, rats. I read that somewhere a long time ago, and meant to try to research it, but never did. Bitch remembers all kinds of obscure, esoteric stuff that washes out of my mind like muddy water and then she quizzes me like she's some kind of mistress of secret knowledge and I'm an idiot. She forgets that I have taught her everything she knows, or rather exposed her to it. So what if she remembers things when I was half asleep or entirely asleep, big deal. Dreams don't count.

"Leave me alone," I demand. "I have to work on my court appeal."

"Go ahead. But you ought to look at that copy of the Stockholm syndrome that Harriet Nahanee gave you before she died. She was onto something, you know."

I ignore her parting shot and get out the court transcripts my family had to pay twelve thousand dollars for in order to appeal my trial two years earlier that ended in a sentence of ten months which I have already served. But I can't focus on the transcripts. Is Bitch right? Am I, a mother of eight, grandmother of eight and great grandmother of one, actually a man...or a female version of a man as all women are female versions of men? Oh, baloney. Women have massive amounts of estrogen and other female stuff that makes us markedly different from men. My ancient female innards are post baby-making but they are still there and they house reservoirs of female hormones that still feed my brain and body. But yes, I have to admit, in post-menopausal women, at least those who are not on hormone replacement, there must be more balance between the genders; the lessening of estrogen and other female hormones creates a more equal proportion with the naturally occurring male hormones in any post-menopausal female body.

So maybe the post-menopausal woman is the crowning glory of nature's achievement. Between the reproductive woman and the male of any age, the post-menopausal woman has the most perfect hormonal balance. But I ask myself, what good does it do us, even if true, if we can't think outside our culture? Our culture is male. Is it as Bitch claims and that I, too, am what she claims ...an artificial male? At least culturally? That I am actually an old drag queen, and most young women on this earth in reality are young drag queens, that is, females conditioned to become compliant male-identified women instead of the fierce female warriors they actually are, or at least were? After centuries of indoctrination do women know that if we refuse to be sweetened by the cultural force of male power demands then we will face the consequences of expulsion from society altogether, especially old women? So to survive in this culture, just as all old women must, I too am obliged to take the pose of the sweet, gentle grandmother in order to be accepted by any legitimate agency in society. And this, of course, is also what elder balanced women had to do historically in order to escape the witch burnings that happened when they actually tried to offer opposition to the stupidities of both young and old unbalanced men in the religious Inquisitions of the past.

Oh, rats. This is way too complicated. It makes my head ache. Damn that copy of the Stockholm syndrome Harriet gave me. She gave it to me before she was hauled off to prison while I was still on trial. I do have a copy of it somewhere. And Harriet told me things were different, even in her living memory, when she was a child back on the Pacheedaht First Nation reserve on Vancouver Island. Until the church people came and stole her and the other children in the village away to residential school she said women were respected in her village. It was after residential school, when the children were grown, that things began to fall apart. Then too many native men, taking their cues from white men, began to drink and beat their women. And some of the women began to drink, too, and like the men, unused to an addictive substance that was poison to their systems, began to falter in their sense of direction.

I can't find the paper but I remember that Harriet had compared the Stockholm syndrome to Indians trying desperately to deal with white people (Harriet referred to herself as Indian; she claimed that the term "First Nations" was condescending; I honour her in this and refer to First Nations people as Indians even if I am accused of being racist.) And I agree with Harriet's correlating the Stockholm syndrome with the Indians' first contact with white people on these shores. But I also know what Bitch is hinting at. Bitch wants to reference the Stockholm syndrome to the psychological condition of women of all races trying desperately to deal with men of all races. I'm not going there. At least not at this point.

It is now March 3, 2009. The stock market bit the dust and is floating in the six thousand range. I can smell the sulphur flames of corruption and fiscal irresponsibility erupting deep within the country's economic innards. I am getting seriously worried about the ability of the human race to rise above the economic feces that capitalism is in the process of expelling. If it's all determined to fall down in a colossal mess before my own demise, then I have to think seriously about the transition period from capitalism to whatever the hell is coming next.

Security. I worry about violence, as do so many other women. Law and order is already breaking down in my city under the force of drug gangs and homelessness which are the end result of governmental and corporate corruption. I want a good long break from the city. I long for nature.

Marian's first bid on the old dream house in the Valley wasn't accepted, but with the rewiring done, she might now think about making a higher offer. We're going back on Saturday for a final look. Marian is antsy. She is in a relationship that will surely suffer some stresses if she moves so far away, as her significant other must, for many reasons, remain in the city. Choice time. But I am obliged to the universe to assume that all can be overcome. Yes, we can. Oh, yes, we can. But in case we can't, we must make a Plan B.

"I'll help you," Blue Belle volunteers, waving a new freshly-ironed hanky to get my attention. "That is, if you like."

"No, I don't like," I snap. "You don't know anything about...well, the basic necessities of life. You've been pampered all of your life by some man or other who saw to it that you had all of the necessities. Well, we don't have a man now. All we have is...dare I say it...each other."

"Yes, dare to say it," Blue Belle sniffs. "You know I am not averse to sacrifice. The Bible teaches sacrifice and selflessness and even if you do think that only the old witch helps you when you're in trouble, I'll thank you to remember that I helped you, too, in prison when some of the other prisoners got on your nerves and I counseled you to be patient and kind..."

I pause and consider her offer. Blue Belle can be helpful at times. She has a way with pleasing phrases. People like her. But I also know how she abhors snow and that she really doesn't want to move. She longs for the hot suns of southern Louisiana even if the old house we are bidding on reminds her of ancient southern houses. So fearful of sabotage, I gently close her door.

This time Marian and I spent a good part of the afternoon back at our dream house for a thorough second and third look. It is charming. And very roomy. And while old, it is upgraded. But could we actually manage such a large house? After all, even should we purchase the house Marian wouldn't be able to spend much time in it for at least eight months because of the field work for her PhD thesis. It would just be me and Rhodes to start with. And Hoffman. Of course, Marian would leave her cat with us. And if I got lonely for whatever reason there was always Blue Belle and Bitch.

So we took the plunge. Marian submitted another offer on the house last week, quibbled a bit with an exchange of counter offers and then accepted the owners' final counter offer. Now we must wait for inspections and such. Daughter Rose Mary, while helpful with the process, wonders if we are biting off more than we can chew. We may have taken leave of conventional wisdom about why two women, one very elderly, should want to be burdened by the upkeep of such a large old house but then I have never been a conventional person, nor has Marian. For that matter, none of the eight children I have given birth to, held close, and raised (including the one now saying this house might not be such a good idea), have been very conventional themselves, whatever conventional means these days. But who knows whether anything one wants to do is a good idea or not until one actually does it, excluding, of course, suicide. I draw the line there.

I have resumed home schooling Rhodes, as I have done since he was in fourth grade. He has dyslexia. My mother home schooled me, as she recognized the peculiarities of dyslexia by trying to teach her younger sister who also had a learning disability. And this morning, part of Rhodes' lesson is listening to the news. It isn't pretty. Mass shootings in Germany; some guy went berserk and killed a crowd of people in a youth camp (okay, a case could be made here for suicide if it happened to the shooter before the shootings). This is so disturbing we give up lessons for the day. I try to enter into conversation with Rhodes about such crazy actions, but really, what is there to say except that the man is mad?

The most unfortunate thing in the world is for a child to lose his or her mother. At four Rhodes didn't understand why his mother had died. I cared for him for those first months until his father could arrange to take him to Victoria to live with him. I followed in order to be close to Rhodes. At first it wasn't too bad. I had Rhodes frequently during those early years. But Rhodes's father and I live on different planets and there were too many disagreements around child care. Add to the mix that I was jailed several times over environmental issues. By the fourth grade Rhodes wasn't doing well in school and I remembered only too well my own struggles as a child. So Rhodes' father agreed that we should take him out of school and I would home school him. And this went fairly okay for a number of years. At least until Rhodes' father met a women that he was serious about.

Rhodes was not crazy about this turn of events. He began acting out. He liked his new step mother well enough; it was the new baby coming that at first threw him into a nose dive. But after his little brother's arrival Rhodes seemed to adjust. He now had a regular family. His father took over his home schooling. Rhodes was now big enough to manage the ferry by himself for visits so I moved to Vancouver.

But things didn't work out with Rhodes' new family life. His step mother packed it in after a couple of years and left. She took the new little brother with her and I took up home schooling Rhodes again. So there began a period of frequent ferry rides between Victoria and Vancouver. The stays with me became ever longer until Rhodes just forgot to go back to Victoria and made his primary home with me. But through all of this emotional turmoil, his education suffered greatly. Curiously enough, or maybe not so curiously, Rhodes' knowledge of computers and how electricity and motors and robots work has increased enormously. Just turning eighteen, Rhodes buys old computers and electrical products from thrift stores and garage sales and fixes them for resale. And we are catching up on school work. In September he will enter the adult school system. This new old house will be good for him, too. So we will see what the house inspector has to say. Only then will we know for sure the deal is on.

A week later, the inspector has spoken and we are somewhat closer to the house but it still isn't a done deal. There seem to be a couple of problem areas. While the structure of the house is basically sound after a hundred and fifteen years of being lived in, loved, hated, pounded on, added on, torn up, its guts operated on and replaced, the attic still needs more stuffing and there are a couple of joists underneath the house where the furnace lives that need replacing. Okay, who is going to do this repair work, us or them? Marian will try to get this question answered tomorrow. Hopefully it's them. However, even if it is, this means more delays. But at least some members of the family are gradually coming on board after actually seeing the house. Daughters Susan and Margaret Elizabeth are impressed, as are Rose Mary and her husband Jim. And Rhodes is excited. His bedroom to be is large with nothing of mine having to be stored in the closet or under his bed. Marian wanted to talk personally to the inspector so they all went for a look last Saturday.

I stayed home, having a second visitation by the bug that settled into my inner regions after my brother died. This particular visit of gastronomical misery had arrived a few days before. I thought I had managed to beat it back by not eating anything but a banana and drinking a coke for two days. And never mind tirades against Coca Cola. I turned against their rotten corporate practices many years ago. Aside from devastating many parts of the third world's water supply, and contributing mightily to obesity and tooth decay in the Western world, Coca Cola has something else to account for that has escaped serious medical attention.

Aside from all its other sins, Coke apparently contains some ingredient that evidently can wipe out whole colonies of harmful bacteria in the human gut, probably along with whole colonies of beneficial ones, within twenty-four hours. As one rabid anti-coke gentleman told me many years ago, sure Coke can kill intestinal bacteria; why they've made experiments where Coke can cut through train tracks when applied steadily over a couple of weeks. I took the train story with a grain of salt; however I have come to the conclusion that the Coke people should not be allowed to advertise their wares as a harmless soft drink. Coke should be kept behind the counter in drug stores and sold only by prescription and that only when nothing else stops the flow of discontent.

Thinking myself well, I started eating again. The bug had not been vanquished; it was only hiding, waiting for the weakness in an early declaration of victory to reappear. (I was reminded of the "mission accomplished" sign in Iraq after the US invasion.) Rhodes, anxious to attend the trip planned for the following day to Merryland ate, drank, and munched down four cloves of raw garlic to ward off any chance of gastric contamination from his grandmother. And the garlic seemed to work. He didn't get sick. But riding in a closed car the following day with Rhodes' still pungent smell (in spite of showering and antiseptic gargling) caused some complaints from his female relatives. However, this morning as I am still in the grips of the anti-gut gods, Rhodes insists I try the garlic cure.

Well, son of a gun. By the end of the day I'm not cured but my stomach no longer seems at odds with my will to live. Two days later I'm feeling almost okay. Time to look at emails.

There's the symposium on prostitution and human trafficking at the university on Thursday. I'm speaking at an anti-Olympic rally Monday evening and have three out of town book readings in April. And if this house comes through it means giving notice at the end of the month, and suffering people coming to look at my apartment. Not to mention actually packing. And trying to get ready for May's court appeal at the same time. It's too much.

Which is the story of my life. Too much. Too many husbands. And eight kids. Although I can't honestly say the kids were too much. They were all so interesting to me, then and now. It was the husbands. The husbands took too much time and attention away from the kids. Societies (read men who wrote the Bible, the Koran, the Bhagavad Gita, the whatever, and who take care of the old boy's financial clubs around the world) have insisted that the man-woman, husband-wife bond is the priority bond. Which make husbands (or partners) the biggest kids in the house. Women should not be crucified in this way. It's all horribly wrong.

Kids should be the priority. Women know this in their guts. It's in our DNA. Even if women opt not to have children, their DNA understands that a society based primarily on the needs of men cannot be anything but corrupt. This is why women have to take over the world. I catch my breath. My God. This is out of the mouth of Bitch. And speaking of the devil, her tasseled head appears around the doorway to her rooms.

"I can't believe it," Bitch chortles and does a little soft shoe shuffle over to my space. "You're getting it. You're finally getting it."

"All right, just calm down," I answer. "This doesn't mean I'm completely convinced. It's just that ...well, the evidence is kind of overwhelming. I just heard about this goofy situation where the Attorney General of British Columbia is meeting with an official of Mexico to try to work together on sharing information about the drug cartels in order to stop gang wars. If either of them had any information about the gangs that was likely to work, one would think they would be using it. What are they going to share? Besides frustration? Parts of Mexico are becoming so lawless some members of their police are applying for asylum in the US. And I'm not so sure anymore that government officials anywhere are really scandalized by drug violence."

"Scandalized by drug violence?" Bitch repeats mockingly. "The reason politicians won't legalize drugs is because there is too much money in illegal drugs. It's one of the biggest money makers in the world. Politicians know this. So do financiers. And the police. They all pretend it ain't so. And some of them have a finger in the pie the world over. And you know what else is in that pie? Blood. Blood of innocents. The blood of children. But these assholes claim they have to keep the black market for drugs going so the children won't be corrupted. What a bunch of jerks! And this is what women are supposed to admire, these fucking men who don't give a damn about anything but their own power and pleasure."

"I wish you wouldn't use that kind of language," Blue Belle pipes up, hovering around the only partially drawn curtains to her quarters. She's obviously been eavesdropping. "It's so crude," she goes on. "Were you raised in a barn?"

"Don't get cutesy with me," Bitch snaps, addressing Blue Belle directly. "My ancestry is golden. Some of my ancestors were sitting on the rocks on these shores watching your bunch of murdering ancestors land."

"My ancestors didn't all come from England." Blue Belle tosses her head. "Some of them came from..." she begins and then hesitates. She obviously isn't sure she wants to go into her ancestry. She knows her maternal grandparents came from England several generations back but because of family secrecy surrounding the grandparents on her father's side, her ancestry has never been very clear to her.

"They came from hell," Bitch finishes for her. Blue Belle sniffs.

"You're only part native, the rest is French and the French weren't exactly sterling in their conduct when they came over here. Or even over there," Blue Belle offers in rebuttal.

"There... where?" Bitch demands.

"Europe. Before the revolution the French upper classes were the most decadent of peoples and the peasants the poorest and when the French came to this country they took to slaughtering Indians like it was a new sport and..."

"Okay, that's enough," I interrupt before Bitch can again remind Blue Belle that one set of Blue Belle's grandparents were actually converted German Jews which Blue Belle would, in her partial ignorance of the matter, hotly deny.

"Fine," Bitch responds readily enough, turning away from Blue Belle. "Just try to sneak a peek at the Stockholm syndrome, okay? Harriet wanted you to study it."

I agree just to get rid of her. I have to write something around the need to keep the anti-Olympic spirit alive. Bitch leaves and I look at Blue Belle.

"Tell me," I say. "You actually agree with Bitch about not legalizing prostitution. But do you agree that drugs should be legalized?"

Blue Belle pooches out her bottom lip. "It's a contradiction," She says after a moment. "The two really aren't the same, yet it seems so. I mean, if it would be better to legalize drugs in order to stop the killing and corruption because of the black market around them, wouldn't legalizing prostitution also stop the mistreatment of prostitutes?"

"Would it?" I ask.

Blue Belle shakes her head. "I don't really think so. Men can be such beasts. Some would think that if prostitution is legal, then certain types of men would consider it a green light to use more violence on women, not less. Certain types of men."

"Certain types of men," I repeat, keeping my voice neutral.

"Yes," Blue Belle continues. "Certainly not all of them are like Witch describes. There are good men out there."

"And do you have a good one?" I ask innocently. I am curious about Blue Belle's thoughts around her relationships; sometimes she seems prudish to the point of being asexual.

Apparently startled by my question she stares at me for a brief moment, her blue eyes clouding with confusion.

"I don't know what you are asking," she says finally in a quiet, brittle voice. With a nervous little gesture she soothes down the pale blue organdy skirt with a soft, white hand. "I have to go now."

I stare after her retreating figure as she slips back inside her pale blue curtained rooms. Blue Belle rarely leaves before I dismiss her. Okay. Whatever. I do have to get to work.

CHAPTER THREE
Bluc Belle and Bitch Mix it Up

THE ANTI-OLYMPIC RALLY WENT OKAY IN SPITE OF THE RAIN
and cold. As usual, I discarded the speech I had formulated in my head and
just went with the crowd. I talked about Orwell's *Animal Farm* and the role
played by the pigs in the story and related this to the government officials
inside the trade centre with the corporate sponsors of the Olympics. Not
very nice, but Bitch urged me on, saying this was probably my last jab at the
local Olympic destroyers of the universe as we are leaving Vancouver. We
will be moving next month into the dreamy old house in the country village
on Vancouver Island. So in my speech I didn't try to hold back in my con-
demnation of Gordon Campbell and VANOC and the corporate structure.

But doggone, it was cold parading around in front of the Trade Centre
at Waterfront Station holding a blown up photo of Harriet Nahanee protesting at Eagleridge Bluffs. Harriet is my hero. For me she personified
bravery, in her life and untimely death. As an elderly first Nations woman
she struggled against racism, sexism, ageism, and what she considered the
treachery of her chiefs in making deals to trade away traditional Squamish
land. She fought to the very last. We stood together on Eagleridge Bluffs,
trying to save it. We didn't. Harriet was sent to serve out her fourteen-day
sentence in the hell hole of the Surrey Pre-trial Centre. I knew what it was
like; I had been held there before while waiting to see a judge. It was a
holding prison with not enough of anything including blankets, and the
air conditioning was left on full blast. Harriet caught pneumonia and died
shortly after her release. I speak of her whenever the opportunity arises.
But it was so rainy and cold at the protest today even the portrait of Harriet

I was carrying couldn't keep me warm. Aside from half a dozen other niggling little signs of getting old I find I am sympathizing more with Blue Belle's aversion to the cold.

I don't believe in burning bridges but there is one I burned; forty-three years ago I burned this sucker, to be exact. And I will not be enticed back to the States by a new half-black president. The other half of him is white. And that half is revving up the conflict in Afghanistan and Pakistan. This white half evidently cannot resist trying to make the entire world American. The only thing that will stop this will be the total collapse of the American dollar. Which may come sooner than later, at least according to some writers.

At the moment Obama is throwing good money after bad by pouring trillions into the banks and lending institutions. By rewarding lazy corporations with more trillions. Of taxpayer money. While poor people's houses stand empty because of rotten management by their "betters," men who are supposed to understand the monetary situation. Well, actually these men do. They understand how to milk the ailing cow even when it's on its way down and more poor people are being left with the dry tits of corruption and gang wars. In Mexico. The US. Canada. Yes, time to leave the city. The worst is upon us.

We are now into June and Rhodes and I have been in our new old house almost two and a half months. I love it here, except for some excessive dirt biking around the streets that is more than a little annoying. Young boys. Why parents buy kids these things baffles me. They certainly destroy the peace of the neighbourhood. But the old house embraces me like a comfortable friend and the huge wisteria vine hanging onto the back deck railing kisses my face without shame. I don't even know the names of most of the plants and flowers in the yard. But I don't care.

I wake up to the sight of a full grown cedar tree in the middle of the back yard and a huge cherry tree growing through the downstairs deck up to my own little private deckette. Nobody bothers me ~ at least not yet. And because the early morning light pours into my bedroom through uncurtained sliding glass doors I am awake and working on a mug of coffee and the six a.m. news. CBC. Always.

I believe in doing business locally, so now turn to the Vancouver Island CBC radio station instead of Vancouver CBC. But I don't really like either of them much anymore. CBC radio has deteriorated over the years and I don't think it all has to do with cutbacks in funding. Often, much of what the CBC has come to considers news is something fairly trivial in the overall scheme of things. They seem to have lost a sense of what is important in the world, and have become in my opinion, primarily sports reporters. Rick Cluff, the morning show host on Early Edition from Vancouver, used to be a sports reporter. How would we have known that? And this morning on the Island CBC the lead story was about...oh, let's see. It was hockey. Two American teams playing hockey in an American city was the lead story on CBC, our Canadian public broadcasting company. This was more important than what was happening in the Iranian elections, more important than North Korea's sabre rattling, more important than the swine flu pandemic, more important than the news that British Columbia has the highest child poverty rate in Canada. Of course this last is old news. No excitement there. Not even when it was fresh news. But the Stanley Cup? Oh, wow!

"I wish you would stop expecting anything better and get on with it," a familiar voice edged with sarcasm says loftily from the near corner of my bedroom. I look at the owner of the voice. She is slouched in the shabby but comfortable wingback chair the previous owners of the house graciously left behind. From my futon bed where I am propped up drinking coffee she is not a pretty sight. But she isn't entirely unexpected. Bitch frequently visits me now in the early hours. She has taken to arriving with my first few sips of coffee.

I don't rise to Bitch's challenge. It's too early.

"And what did you think of the overnight program about the young unmarried mothers during the sixties?" she asks after a moment.

"I didn't hear it," I lie. I did hear the overnight program. Sort of. I was half asleep.

"Yes, you did," Bitch answers, adopting a patient tone. "About the young unmarried women in Australia who in the sixties gave up their babies for adoption because that was what they were told to do by the Church and by their mothers. And how this one woman went on to marry the young man who impregnated her after she gave the baby up and they had five more children and when the first of these was born how different she found the situation, this time she was doing the same thing, having a baby with the same man but because she was married to him now her room was full of flowers when before it was all shame and secrecy and the state wouldn't help her either because she wasn't married and how she had never recovered fully from that trauma because the female body remembers the baby and the breasts swollen with milk that was for the baby that was stolen away from her no matter how many more she may have ..."

"So?" I ask, when Bitch pauses to take a breath. "Times have changed."

"Really? My, my. There's a brief mention of you in the May 2009 issue of Canadian Reader's Digest. About how you were trying, while in Alouette Prison two years ago, to help out a young mother who was crying because she couldn't stop her infant, who she was allowed to keep in prison with her, from crying. You took the baby and rocked it until a guard came in and told you to stop. The article explained how wonderful the Mother Baby program was..."

"Yes, was," I reply bitterly. "Now the entire program has been cut by Gordon Campbell's BC Liberals.

"Exactly. Under patriarchy the bond between mother and child must always be interfered with one way or another, or else..." Her voice trails away. I don't really want to hear her "or else" but yes, I silently agree, as my own baby bonding was certainly interfered with. When I was married the needs of husbands came first. And during the times I wasn't married and was a working single parent instead, it was food and rent and getting the old car started in the mornings so I could get to work that came first. Health, school, clothes...the very physical needs of children came first. Everything before the children themselves had to come first.

It's a wonder any of my children survived their childhoods. Two of them didn't survive their young adulthood. Why is it that so many young people are getting cancer? But I think I know without Bitch trying to shove the answer down my throat. Children and young people are being poisoned by the profit motive. Stuff. Stuff everywhere made of poisonous materials. Food that is supposed to nourish children but is loaded with compounds to rot their teeth, injure their immune systems, fog their brains, and make them fat. Oh, yes, baby bonding in the Western world is and has been seriously interfered with. We all have to service the man first, personally and/or socially. His needs are encoded in law, are served by the international banks, the political seats of power, entertainment and sport; even if a woman is propped up as a head of whatever, it will be the man she serves, not her own natural constituency, which is children and other women.

"Might I put in a few words here?" Blue Belle asks from the doorway.

"Sure, come on in," I agree. Why not, after all, I'm feeling okay. Last night I slid the thin feather mattress off my futon and slept on it on the floor until earliest morning as I have been wont to do now for some weeks. I like sleeping on the floor. The hardness of the floor underneath the slight feather mattress realigns my spine. Somewhat. As much as anything can realign an eighty-year-old spine that has been through hell and back. But I think my liking for sleeping on the floor in private life greatly contributed to my tolerance for sleeping on the metal bunks at Alouette prison for women.

Blue Belle minces prissily into the room. She seats herself on the ottoman on the opposite side of my bed, away from Bitch. She is dressed for church, wearing a little white off-the-face summer hat with a matching veil and carrying a small straw handbag. At the moment she is busy fluffing down the full organdy skirt of her blue dress; settling the folds to droop around the sides of the ottoman just so. She could be preparing for a photograph.

"Aren't you a little early for church?" I ask. Blue Belle pauses in the business of rearranging her skirts. When she looks over at me her sweet face has a petulant expression.

"I like to go to the early service. And a little church going wouldn't hurt you, either, you know."

"If you will remember," I say rather gently considering the hour and the circumstances, "I gave that up a long time ago."

"And are much the worse for it if I may say so. And you did like church, now didn't you? I know you did. I remember when you liked to go to church..."

"It was the music," I answer defensively. "It was always the music."

"Yes, and you might still play some of it sometimes. You have tapes of your mother and Aunt Sit and Aunt Gladys singing and playing, why don't you play those tapes at least occasionally? Instead of spending so much time with Andrea Dworkin..."

"Oh, Andrea Dworkin isn't the half of it," Bitch breaks in. "Dworkin just scratches the surface. We're after the biological truths Dworkin didn't even consider..." "Shut up!" Blue Belle says fiercely, turning to glare at Bitch, her plump little mouth twisting with agitation. "Just shut up! You're always breaking in when I'm trying to talk. Don't you care about Betty at all? When she's with me she might be considered eccentric but she can function in normal society. When she's with you she's off the wall and nobody will take her seriously..."

Bitch leans forward, bristling.

"And what does that mean, Miss Priss? To be taken seriously by a bunch of dodos? That's what society actually is because that's what the male mind is, including the academic world. Go peddle your little Sunday School tracts that have made your own mind a mush somewhere else..."

I brush them both aside and get up. The remains of my coffee have grown cold and the morning beckons and I must balance these conflicting demons that live inside my head. I will work on it. And I do, so deeply I almost go into a coma trying to think of ways to talk about my concerns in print and over the internet without alienating everybody, men and women alike. I'm not sure it's possible.

But other affairs distract me, rank political affairs. And I mean rank. Stephen Harper is bringing down a federal budget and the federal Liberals in turn are threatening to bring down the government if...well, ostensibly it's primarily over employment insurance. Ignatieff is demanding that Harper change the program to include more people for more time and for more money. And a few other issues. But we'll see what happens. On Friday we are supposed to know how the greats have decided and whether or not we'll face another election.

As the pundits have it, neither party wants an election now. Each thinks they will be more favoured by the body politic down the road a bit. But one or the other will be "snake bit," and I hope it's Harper. My stomach lurches every time I see an image of him, that petulant, stubborn little boy with a mean streak look. In my opinion Ignatieff looks and acts more human but he stated before the last BC provincial election that he hoped the BC Liberals won. As the BC Liberals have more in common with Harper's philosophy, I wonder about Ignatieff's knowledge of politics here. I wish someone would advise him that wanting Gordon Campbell's Liberals to win is like wanting a combination of George Bush and Brian Mulroney to win. Jeez.

Last evening, to rest my fevered mind I turned back to Andrea Dworkin's book Intercourse. I've been reading it off and on. Dworkin scares me. She's getting down and dirty about men. Discounting the frenzied pronouncements by Blue Belle, it is my agreement with Dworkin in certain areas that frightens me. She claims that the very act of intercourse between a man and a woman is an act of occupation and oppression of the female body. There have certainly been times when I have experienced it in this way. But the times when I didn't? When it was pleasurable? Those occasions, Dworkin tells me, were pleasurable because I was out of my mind. During those times, I was so colonized that I had learned to desire having my integrity invaded, that it was a sick thing, sick because my own mind and body didn't belong to me at those times because I had given over my deepest emotions to the colonizer, that it is, in reality, my deepest emotion, at least temporarily, belonged to him. To the colonizer. Interesting.

But for me Dworkin doesn't adequately explain the biological thing, the very fact of nature. However much any woman may dislike the act of penetration in intercourse, this is the way nature has evolved the reproduction of humans just as with all mammals. If God didn't make it this way, and many of us have now jettisoned the male God completely, then evolution did.

Why did evolution make it this way? The only answer has to be: because it works. That's the only reason nature keeps any of her experiments. The fact that humans of both sexes are driven to sexual intercourse because it is encoded in our genes doesn't bother me half as much as why the act of intercourse came to be something that men could use against women, that because women can be fucked, pardon the expression, then it simply follows that this causes men to disrespect women. Even if the fucking is sanctified, with a priest or preacher officiating, with music, dancing, laughing, drinking, and feasting, there is also a profound disquiet, even grief among the older women present at a wedding...the mothers, aunts, older sisters, grandmothers. They often weep. Is it because even in a sanctified marriage all women know the new bride will only experience a year or two at the most of her new husband pretending...pretending what? To be sensitive, gentle, considerate, respectful...in other words to act like a woman? Until the awful truth gradually begins to reveal itself to the unsuspecting young wife that her man is not really simply a male expression of a being much like herself but that he belongs to a whole different clan, the male clan. And the male clan does not respect women in the aggregate.

So the woman, unable or unwilling to totally dish her dreams, doubles up her duties to make it work; she holds an outside job, does most of the housekeeping, all the while carrying the baby growing in her belly, and later takes charge of the baby program and all that entails. Regardless of whether she immediately returns to the work force, she usually returns sooner or later, all the innate separation anxiety based in millions of years of evolution dragging her down while she's still picking up after hubby. Sometimes she packs it in and leaves her first husband only to do it over again, this time hoping for a better deal even though she now has a child or two, and her new man may have a child or two from his first marriage, and they all just hope for the best. If it works it is usually because the woman makes it work, although sometimes the man has been bruised enough from his first marriage to tone down his expectations a bit. All the same his tribe remains the important one, the one that orders society, the one that supports or tolerates the billions of dollars invested in spectator sports, in pornography, in the sex trade, in child abandonment, poverty, prostitution, in drugs, guns, war...

Oh, God, the list is endless. But I don't like to think that nature is so lopsided in her dealings with human females that she deliberately opted for a method of reproduction that is inherently oppressive to women. Why would nature do such a thing? So couldn't the disrespect men evidence toward woman result more from the fact that they have somehow coerced women to believe they have to live with men in order to be safe? Safe from the aggression of other men? But wait a minute... when women die from male violence, or are wounded by the hands of men it is usually by their own male partners. Just because women need men to get pregnant it doesn't necessarily follow that women then have to live with them in a constant, close association. It doesn't follow that because women need men to fertilize their eggs that women must pay for this forever by scrubbing men's houses and cooking their meals and doing their laundry and having sex with them whether they want to or not and pretending to have orgasms while they are doing it. And that women must assume a lower profile, no matter their own talents, so the men can shine. And if an individual man shines brightly enough, the woman may very well have to suffer the humiliation of his having a prettier much younger woman give him a blow job in his office in the White House.

This sexual exchange of services just doesn't compute. Then why do women act as though it does? That question has bugged me for so many years I can't even remember, brought on early by recognizing that while my mother was far superior to my father in very important ways, she almost always acted as if the reverse were true. Unless she was truly provoked by my father and on these rare occasions, the curtains would part briefly on the religious mythologies they both adhered to that made my father head of the family, in direct descent from God the Father, and my mother would severely upbraid him. But when this happened my father would just leave the house and seek the company of other good God-fearing men who knew how silly and capricious women actually were and why did men even bother?

"Oh, but my man isn't like that," the earnest, starry-eyed, in love with love young woman tells me breathlessly. "I've got a good one."

I've heard that so many times I could upchuck. And I want to ask this earnest young woman with stars in her eyes if her man is so good why isn't he out there championing her sex? Why isn't he trying to abolish pornography, human trafficking, prostitution, particularly child prostitution; why isn't he demanding respect for women in film, in the press, why isn't he championing equal pay, better health care for women and children, why isn't her good man saying look, guys, we're spending all of this time and money on spectator sports, why don't we instead try to abolish child poverty which would greatly alleviate the burden on woman including my wife if we split up and she gets stuck with primarily raising the kids?

As long as men sit on their backsides and watch games and drink beer and watch a little porn when they can, and join in the male games of sexist remarks about and to women, then I really want to lay it on the line to my young friend and say, "Honey, you don't necessarily have a good man just because he himself is not raping or pimping, but tolerates it all as a privileged male and is still in good standing with the male tribe. Remember that."

But I don't tell the earnest young women this. I can't. It would take too long. It would take years. She will gradually come to this conclusion herself unless her man is wealthy and her moral fibre becomes so softened by material goodies she gives up thinking altogether.

But here and now there is a development in the male tribe's federal leadership... in the standoff between Harper and Ignatieff. There will be no summer federal election. Instead the barnyard cocks who strut around Ottawa will square off in the fall.

I personally must get focused. Rhodes is away for a week and I have boxes of papers yet to unpack and I will heed Bitch's advice and actually study the paper describing the Stockholm syndrome that Harriet gave me. If I can find it. I think it's on top of the box marked miscellaneous papers.

CHAPTER FOUR
First Sign of Blue Belle Depression

NOPE, CAN'T FIND THE COPY OF THE STOCKHOLM SYN-
drome that Harriet gave me. Have been looking for it sporadically since
yesterday. Wrote a new "missile" and posted it. About how I think it
was, and still remains, men's control of women's reproductive capacity
through the rise of religion and marriage that is the underpinning of global
warming because it has led to overpopulation of the earth. Several negative
responses. From men. One who was a former supporter. Funny how the
winds blow. Just don't step on their blue suede shoes.

"Can we talk?" a soft voice questions at my elbow as I settle myself at the
computer. Something in the tremor of her voice stays my attention. I turn
away from the computer and face Blue Belle. There are faint circles under
her eyes. And her organdy skirt seems somewhat less perky than usual.
But she sits down in the other office chair beside me, the one I don't like
because it's too big for me. Blue Belle is quite lost in it.

"Are you depressed?" I ask. She nods. Even her bouncy blonde curls
seem subdued.

"Yes. Your last missile is enough to depress anybody. How can I go on
with you when you say that all men oppress all women..."

I sigh. "I didn't say that, Blue Belle. What I said is that male control,
which encompasses sexual control of women, has resulted in the overpopulation of the earth..."

"But it's the same thing, isn't it?"

"No. All men can't oppress all women because a lot of men can't or
won't personally force sex on women, or harass, beat, rape, or murder

them. Also children, I might add, usually girls. But all men do partake in the male culture, the male mindset as a whole that defines women as inferior beings who must be managed, whether or not some men do this individually. There are men who recognize that male culture everywhere oppresses women and struggle to understand and deal with this reality in a humane manner. But that doesn't change the male culture and if men are seen as softies they run the risk of being tossed out of the male culture. And then what will they do? There's nowhere for them to go. So they stay inside the male brain, so to speak, for all practical purposes."

Blue Belle straightens in the oversized office chair and stares at me.

"But you're not God. You can't fix the male brain. Nature made their brains the way they are. And there's good in men's brains, too. They understand a lot more than women about practical things like electricity and engineering and how to build boats and airplanes..."

"And bombs," I add. "Nuclear weapons. US drone airplanes that can target and assassinate individual people wherever and whenever they like and also kill everybody standing around them or riding in a vehicle with them."

"But they also make surgical instruments and discover new ways to treat diseases and how to make childbearing easier..."

Our eyes lock, hold. "Don't get me started on that," I warn. Her wide, worried blue eyes yield. She glances away.

"I know you had bad experiences with the first babies," she concedes after a moment. "I remember..."

She breaks off. The smooth skin of her brow creases into a V.

"I don't know why I said that," she says after a moment. "I couldn't remember, could I, because that was you, wasn't it, but well, I know about the clamped down stirrups and how they handcuffed your wrists to the sides of the bed during labour and how the lower part of your body was elevated against all natural inclinations of women trying to get a baby out..."

"Yes," I agree. "It was very similar to being hauled around in a police paddy wagon all handcuffed and leg-ironed. The prison experience certainly put me in mind of having babies during the late forties and fifties and even into the sixties."

"But they don't do that anymore," Blue Belle breaks in earnestly. "With women in labour. Now women can squat or have their babies come out in a pool of warm water..."

"True enough," I concede. "And it's because more women have gone into the medical profession who know more about having babies than male doctors, having had some themselves, and more midwives coming to the fore. But I would like to know how many babies were harmed back then for the doctor's convenience so he wouldn't have to bother to bend over to catch the baby so he could claim to have delivered it. Some doctors weren't even present during the actual birth but claimed they delivered the baby anyway, and charged dearly for it. And I would like to know how many babies were harmed by the use of forceps which became necessary to get the baby out as the doctors had the mother's bum pointed toward the ceiling. How many little tykes in the nursery bore the marks of forceps? Most of them I would wager. And how many mothers were so drugged during the birth process they couldn't even push to help the baby out..."

"All right, enough is enough," Blue Belle breaks in. "They don't do that anymore."

"But they did. They did it to me, with all of my first babies. And I don't forgive them. And the main thing I don't forgive is how the medical profession, the scientific research professions, the physicists, the biologists, entire male-dominated world governments...none of these learned gentlemen thought to wonder what was happening to mother's milk from allowing all manner of herbicides and pesticides and industrial effluent, plastics, flame retardant compounds, detergents, building materials, foams, cleaning agents, shampoos...no, mother's milk was way down the list of their interests, and in their pursuit of excitement, adventure, power, glory, and profit, mother's milk was at the very bottom. The result? Mother's milk is now one of the most polluted foods on the planet. What is this gumbo of pollutants doing to the babies in the long run? Who knows?"

Blue Belle stands up abruptly. "I'm going home. You're giving me a headache. But just remember this. You can't bring about anything important without the will of God and the blessing of God."

I stare at her.

"What?" I screech after a moment.

"You heard me."

She disappears. My heart gives a strange little lurch. That last...that last bit she said. It sounded exactly like Mama. I hang my head, weeping a little inside. Mama, you were such a great mama in so many ways but you were profoundly stupid about men, I whisper to the faded blue indoor-outdoor carpeting of my office floor. On second thought, I think you probably knew quite a lot about men other than just Daddy, who was a law unto himself, but you chose to ignore it. And wanted me to ignore it. I know why. Because it was safer and better for everybody just to ignore male arrogance and stupidity. You worried that if I kept questioning men's right to make all the important decisions and put down women in the process that I would never keep a man. Or be able to stand a man. You kept hoping with each marriage that I would finally settle down and be a regular woman. And you know what, Mama? I hoped for that, too. I really did, especially with the last one.

But when push came to shove, which it eventually did with all four of my husbands, not actually striking me perhaps, but definitely pushing and shoving, my own confidence insisted that I was not born to stand for being treated like an inferior being, and this belief won out. With the last husband, who wasn't at all a bad fellow in many ways (and neither was John, the one before) I made the decision that I would rather live without a mate the rest of my life than be treated as a less intelligent, less talented, and on the whole, lesser being than the man who was supposed to be my partner.

This caused a great deal of suffering for everybody concerned. The kids took the brunt of it. However, for me it was a do or die thing. And even though the children suffered I wanted both sexes to get one message out of all the turmoil: that women were not inferior to men and until women had more say both in and out of the family there would be no peace anywhere. And that's why, Mama, I couldn't be a regular southern woman. This question of supposed male superiority and female inferiority has to be righted before the human race can progress.

Mama doesn't answer. She died ten years ago, on my seventieth birthday. She was going on ninety-seven. Will I make that mark? Maybe, maybe not. My body has taken more of a beating. Mama had just three children. I had eight. And Mama always had a peaceful mind. She didn't doubt her religion, and wasn't caught up in gut-wrenching indecision about what to believe. At least that I knew about. I believe now that doubt stretches one's mind but isn't necessarily good for the body's nervous system. Especially when things go terribly wrong.

My oldest son, oldest child, died five years ago from a brain tumour, at the age of fifty-six; my next to youngest daughter died thirteen years ago from breast cancer at the age of thirty. My deceased son was an electrical engineer, an artist, and a philosopher. His articles, published in science magazines, tackled the question of artificial intelligence and why computers would never be able to think; he wrote about evolution and was writing a book on how human intelligence is born through volition, through feelings, when he died. My deceased daughter was a ballet dancer. Barbara Ellen begged for ballet lessons when she was only four years old and took summer classes at the Canadian National Ballet School. Her dream was to choreograph ballets that would include different ethnic dances. She particularly wanted to choreograph a dance incorporating native dances performed by native children of the West Coast.

Both my son and daughter were cut down before their dreams could be realized. I have six children left and I worry for them every day. Cancer is epidemic and governments do nothing, or very little, about the pollutants that cause cancer in the young and the middle aged. They have allowed the corporations who fill their political coffers to spew out pollutants in hundreds, even thousands, of products that cause cancer and damage the reproductive systems of young people, without thought or responsibility.

Instead of demanding governments take responsibility and address of the issue of cancer-causing pollutants, women in Canada and the US pin or tie pink ribbons everywhere and run to raise more money for research organizations that are, in my opinion, cancer pimps. These organizations will never research the real causes of cancer because they are largely funded by agencies that cause cancer. Women must march with rage in their hearts and spit in the face of the politicians instead of running in circles with pink ribbons; start yelling the truth instead of smiling; demand cancer prevention instead of simply trying to manage cancer treatment, which makes the cancer industry even richer.

The ringing of the phone interrupts my thoughts. It's Marian. She will arrive next week. Marian's PhD work in Medical Anthropology involves research inside hospitals. Yesterday she gave a talk to a committee of nurses and doctors working in the Palliative Care units where she has been researching. It was stressful for her as her particular field is new, and she wanted to emphasize the relevance of her research. She seems pleased by the response.

Rhodes has been visiting his Aunt Sue (my oldest daughter) and her family in Vancouver and will come home with Marian. They will bring two of Marian's friends with them. Rose Mary, who still lives in Ucluelet on the West Coast, will be here with her family plus the family dog and after that (or is it before?) Monika, my good friend and supporter will visit for several days with her husband and stepdaughter. So I have only this one week before the onslaught begins and I plan just to ignore the gardens until help arrives.

I may have to stay inside the house for a week in order to actually ignore the gardens. The weather is rainy and warm and things outside are just exploding; I'm almost afraid to go out there. The downstairs deck threatens: the huge wisteria vine tries to suck me into its dense foliage every time I open the back door and the lavish grape vine tendrils on the far side of the deck wave frantically in the air; having succeeded in climbing the railings they now seek more places to anchor in order to spread out. I give them lots of room on my way to my deck chair.

The groping vines seem to sense the warmth of my solid body. I fear if I sit close to them they will start sending tendrils around my ankles. Or worse, my neck. And when I step off the deck there are plants and flowers all around the house and covering the fence and I don't know a fraction of their names. They too have become totally irresponsible. Not content with growing upwards out of sight they hover along the walkways, obscuring the paths. The cherry tree is so fruitful it is attracting attention from all manner of birds and insects. The berry bushes are trying to spread all over, also growing upward, reaching for what? The sun itself? No, enough is enough. Some of this stuff will have to be cut down to size. We're not in the jungle business here. I have told Marian to bring at least one machete when she comes back.

But until then, I have one free week to write. If Bitch and Blue Belle will just leave me alone. But I feel uneasy about Blue Belle. She gets so upset with me.

I used to love Blue Belle. There was a time when she made me very happy. This was long ago, right after the end of the Second World War, during the six years, more or less, of my first marriage. I had two darling little boys, and while there were some health problems with the second one, it was all manageable. We lived in a modest house of our own, in a reasonably good part of town. The husband I had married at sixteen was ten years older, very handsome, and made a living for us all with his own small construction company. I went to church and took the children. My husband usually begged off. He wasn't an unbeliever; he just liked to relax on Sunday mornings. So he claimed.

Like Blue Belle, I loved church. I loved the singing and the good fellowship. I too wore organdy dresses and little off the face hats with veils and pressed my crisp, white gloves against my Bible and got up and testified about how much the Lord had blessed me and my loved ones. I learned how to do this in Daddy's revival meetings years before. After church my husband would pick us up and we would drive over to my parent's house for Sunday dinner. Monday morning my husband would be out of the house early and wouldn't return until late in the evening.

I honestly didn't question my husband being away so much. He was the man, the provider; he had to work hard to pay the bills. He was also the first man I had ever dated as Daddy wouldn't let any boys around my own age even step into the house unless it was for some kind of prayer meeting. But I was happy enough with the situation of my marriage. I was extremely ignorant. I only did one thing somewhat different from the other very young, very ignorant white southern housewives I knew. I read. Non-stop. Trash novels, history books, how-to books; it was all good. Mama home schooled me until I married and I had developed the habit of independent reading. So during the long days I played endlessly with my little boys and visited with other wives in the neighbourhood. None of the wives I knew worked outside the home. In the afternoons while the boys were napping I got out my latest books.

But a couple of months after my third son was born my pretty little situation became mercilessly, irrevocably, irredeemably ugly. My husband seduced a very young woman, who aside from being underage, was within the defined boundaries of family...family being recognized up to at least five times blood removed. Family pressure to leave my husband was absolute. In those days if a young single girl lost her virginity with any man, much less a married man, it drastically lessened her chances of receiving a marriage proposal from a single man with assets enough to support a family. Marriage was the only game in town for any young woman who wanted children. Well, I already had my children. And I was truly furious. I left my husband, taking the children with me. My husband begged, pleaded with me not to divorce him, to give him time to make amends, when he saw he couldn't actually lie his way out of what he had done.

My husband needn't have worried about my getting an immediate divorce. This was Louisiana, in the fifties. When I went to court to try for a divorce the judge thought I was making a mistake in leaving my husband over such a trivial matter, one that I couldn't actually prove as there was no eye witness to the deed, as was required by Louisiana law in those days. He also thought I should stay with my husband for the children's sake, considering their tender ages. The judge ordered me back into the domestic domicile. I refused.

It wasn't until I moved to Arizona with the children, along with my parents, that I managed to get a divorce after waiting a year. And when I had calmed down enough to analyze my own feelings about my husband's treachery, I recognized that my fury wasn't so much from wounded pride but outrage that my husband had been so stupid. Something had gone seriously wrong with his decision making if he truly cared for me and the kids as he claimed. How could I have lived with such a stupid man?

Blue Belle agreed with my leaving my first husband. But she didn't agree with my marrying the second time. I didn't either, a year and a half later. I now had a little baby girl to add to my family of boys and Blue Belle, like Mama, was seriously worried. Still, they approved of my third husband as he was young, educated, made enough money to support me and the kids, and seemed eager to ingratiate himself with the family. Again, it was all good. We lived well and in relative harmony. Blue Belle and I started back to church again with the children. Again, without my husband. But this one wasn't a hypocrite like my first husband, he was a physicist and an atheist. I thought him interesting, and I downplayed his atheism with the rest of the family. It was at a meeting at a Unitarian Fellowship in Virginia in 1963 that Bitch first came and sat beside me. And introduced herself. Sort of.

Actually, Bitch was introduced to me by the woman giving the lecture that Sunday. She was a feminist. An older woman, her voice was calm and authoritative, her message clear: women were systemically oppressed by male institutions. I listened, astonished. Oh, I had read a bit about feminism but it hadn't really stuck. There was just no way any kind of feminist theory could sink into any woman's head in Louisiana...why, that went totally against the Bible and catering to your man and a woman had to please her man in the bayou...churn out that gumbo and sweet potato pie so your man will take good care of you and the kids.

But the gumbo and sweet potato pie didn't always cut ti e mustard as many a southern woman found out to her surprise and disgust. Me, for one. Anyway, we weren't in Louisiana at the time I first became aware of Bitch. We were in Virginia, where my husband had been hired as a research physicist at NASA. And while historically Virginia had been a slave state, with most of the prejudice and racial injustice still hanging on, the entire state had not been born again, like in Louisiana. I thought there must be more born again Christians in Louisiana than anywhere else in the USA, maybe in the whole world. And I was sure that anything like this Unitarian fellowship I had accidentally discovered would not have been allowed to exist anywhere in Louisiana...why, this woman was talking about legalizing abortion, for God's sake. As I listened, enthralled, Bitch moved a little closer to me in the church pew. I didn't pay her any mind. Not then. But in the days, months, years that followed, Bitch would pop up from time to time. I couldn't see her very clearly at first and she didn't stay very long, just brief little visits, long enough to leave me feeling irritated and uneasy. Blue Belle came relatively often and it seemed that she had always been there.

Now it seems the tide has turned. Bitch is the favoured companion. Is it my age? Or the times?

Michael Jackson died two days ago. The whole world seems to be in mourning. This is ridiculous. The man was being reviled as a pedophile and there was all the weird stuff around whitening his skin and the feminization of his nose but because he could sing and dance and had the grace to die young, suddenly he is a musical saint. But really...what were his songs about that could have relevance for women? What are any of the pop songs sung by popular artists anywhere that could have relevance for women except maybe some of the Dixie Chicks songs? But I have to set aside worries about Blue Belle and the strange mass behaviour around the death of Michael Jackson. There is company at our house.

Marian and Rhodes have brought two women with them for a short visit. Marian's friends are lesbians. They are discussing their wedding plans that include being married in our back garden. Romance is in the air. Rhodes is enamoured of my oldest daughter's stepdaughter and as there is no blood kin, everybody seems to approve. But I am uneasy about the attraction as it seems to be intense on Rhodes' part. He is only eighteen and still more boy than man. However, the young woman in question is a year and half older and more woman than girl. So we'll see.

Three days later, Friday, the 3rd of July, the old house is still busy with my kith and kin. At the moment, the house crew has gone out to test the riding trails on their mountain bikes. Marian has decided to buy Rhodes a mountain bike outright and let him pay her back when he gets a job. I have reservations. I think Rhodes should earn the money first. But I am persuaded otherwise. He is so engrossed with the computer. Rhodes makes videos, electronic music; he is learning how to manipulate electronic images. He could use more exercise; the sooner the better.

The company has distracted me from looking for Harriet's paper and from crossing swords with a blogger who has reprinted an article from a Catholic newspaper that links my name to another activist woman. One who is pro-life, anti-woman, male and Catholic identified. God, how I hate this. I wouldn't ordinarily leave a comment on anybody's blog or web page but I just couldn't let this go unchallenged because by its slant, the article seems to imply that the anti-choice woman and I are in sympathy with each other's aims, or at least that I am in sympathy with hers. So I answer. Stupidly. He (of course the blogger is a he) answers, even more stupidly. I decide that I won't answer his stupid answer with yet another stupid answer.

When Marian left along with her friends, Rhodes stayed behind with me. He will find a job and take some math courses. And he likes to cook. For our evening repast Rhodes laid out the left over salmon cream sauce Marian had made earlier along with fresh pasta and green beans from the farmer's market. I made a cherry pudding with cherries from our own tree. After dinner clean up Rhodes opts for a bike ride. I settle down in the office to do a bit of work until he returns, my door closed to block the noise from two young dirt bikers going round and round the paved roads in our neighbourhood. They obviously don't know the location of any actual dirt to ride in. And they also obviously have parents who don't give a damn about the rest of the world.

But Bitch announces herself with excited, frenetic knocking. As soon as I let her in I suspect that she has discovered something new concerning how men are going down the tube. I have this suspicion because she is waving a fistful of papers as she enters. She plumps herself down in the big office chair and rolls it over next to my smaller one.

"Statistics," she says cheerfully.

I lean back in my chair and look at her. She's so very old and rumpled. More so than usual. She is wearing a short, dark, dusty top and the jeans with the hole in the knee. Her dyed red and green hair is standing on end showing an inch and half of white roots. She could be a bag lady. She could be an ancient Roma woman cast out from the caravan for disobeying all known Roma laws. She could be a chicken hawk, the kind Mama used to scream at for swooping down and snatching up one of her newly hatched "biddies." She could be the "Wild Woman" of ancient Indian lore who would frighten children and sometimes eat them if they stayed out after dark. She could be...but she isn't. Bitch is educated. She can read statistical charts.

"Look at this," she says, shoving the papers on my desk in front of me. I look. It is a graph of the ratio of males to females in all of the countries of the world. Bitch directs my attention to several of the countries with a black marker. "See this? And it's right from the horse's mouth...JAMA, the Journal of the American Medical Association. Look, headlines..."

I look. Bold black letters: REDUCED RATES OF MALE TO FEMALE BIRTHS IN SEVERAL INDUSTRIAL COUNTRIES.

"But we knew that already, didn't we?" I ask. "That's old news."

"Well, it's not generally known now, is it?" Bitch snaps. "I listen to CBC radio the same as you. They don't talk about it. This disappearing male thing is occurring in Canada...you'd think there would be more discussion about it."

"They do talk about the drop in male births in the Sarnia region...you know, Chemical Valley in Ontario," I venture.

"For God's sake. Of course I know! We used to live there, remember? And we refused to die there which is what would have happened had we stayed, the place was so polluted it was impossible to draw a breath that wasn't half poison gas and the man of the house refused to move away..."

"Let's don't go into that," I interrupt.

"Okay, but listen...this sudden drop in male births is happening not just in Sarnia, but in the US and Sweden, Germany, Norway, Finland, Denmark, the Netherlands and some countries in South America. But the really, really weird thing is this...in some parts of China, India, and South Korea the opposite thing is happening...there are more boys being born."

I look at Bitch. Her sunken dark eyes are fairly gleaming with excitement.

"It's because these three countries have a real thing for boys and abort the females if they can as soon as they find out the sex," she continues. "Of course they don't all do that... but enough do so that it's seriously screwing up the sex ratio. Why don't you get that book we heard about... you know, the one called Bare Branches. I even found the authors for you. Two women. Their names are Valerie M. Hudson and Andrea Den Boer. They describe exactly what is happening in parts of China and India with so many boys being born in ratio to girls..." Bitch demands, nudging me with her skinny elbow.

"It's on order," I say. I don't tell her about the other book I have on order. The one called Evolution's Rainbow. I don't want to upset Blue Belle with this bit of information in case she is eavesdropping on my conversation with Bitch. Or perhaps notices the book title when it gets here. She does that sometimes. I'm just a little bit careful because Evolution's Rainbow is about sex, the sex of people, animal, plants, all living things and how sex is much more diverse than is commonly acknowledged. Evolution's Rainbow is written by Joan Roughgarden, a transgendered woman. Blue Belle is very uncomfortable with raw sex discussions even in a clinical presentation. She shrinks from Andrea Dworkin's work as if Dworkin were the devil.

Dworkin must have been very familiar with that reaction as she wrote about sex so much and in such blunt, provocative terms. Where on earth did the woman get the nerve? She died in her sleep of myocarditis, April 9, 2005, age 58. So young. She should have lived longer to explain the contradictions in her theories to me.

"I have to work," I say in a firm voice to Bitch. "Take your papers away and let me look at my own stuff. "

Bitch disappears with an offended jerk of her head. But she has reminded me of something with her presence. I haven't located Harriet's copy of the Stockholm Syndrome. I must search for it again.

Days later I still haven't found Harriet's paper. I'm outside watching a humming bird fly into the dense foliage of the cherry tree. There are enough cherries for all. In fact, there are too many blasted cherries. They sit in thick clusters high on the tree. Out of reach. Rhodes and I have picked all the ones we can safely reach off my second storey deck and off the main deck downstairs. Ripe cherries fall from the tree onto the decks, leaving gooey blobs with seeds that stick to the deck flooring. But the ones we can reach before they fall are absolutely delicious. We do have the most beautiful garden. It's a joy to sit outside, to work among the flowers, the bees, the raspberry and blackberry bushes, the robins and jays and humming birds.

High summer, the middle of July. Marian left this morning after a three day visit. Just before dinner Rhodes and the two women who are planning to marry in our garden went for a short bike ride in the forest. Rhodes came home bleeding and bruised, but nothing too serious. After first aid was administered we all sat down to the shrimp fry that was getting cold. During dinner, the conversation switched from biking to the work of one of the women. A police officer, our guest was familiar with domestic violence and the conversation went in that direction. But the interesting thing to me was that Rhodes seemed to listen intently to what she was saying.

Rhodes is a rather quiet fellow. He especially shies away from talking about gender issues. However, he admires our guest for her athletic prowess and listens to what she has to say on prostitution, rape, and violence in general. Thank goodness her opinions more or less equal mine. Of course I would have given them short shrift if they hadn't. And Blue Belle didn't have a fit, at least one I was privy to, in fact she didn't even surface when I retired for the evening. I think Blue Belle was perhaps still bummed out from her performance the last night Marian and Justin were here.

Rhodes had been busy that particular evening. Only Marian, Justin and I sat down to watch the video I had selected. It was The Prophet, written and directed by Robert Duvall, who also played the lead role. The story speaks to my Louisiana childhood. The preacher (Robert Duvall's role) reminds me a lot of my own father. But it wasn't just that passionate, wacky kind of preaching that Daddy reached for, it was the singing, the fellowship, the spirit of the thing that is, and was, so much a part of the Louisiana life that I knew.

All the other movies I've seen that have presented life in the southern states in days gone by, particularly in the Deep South, might as well have been portraying life on another planet as far as I was concerned. The South I grew up in was composed of poor black and white farmers with small holdings, the whites only being marginally better off than the blacks. And religion was an integral part of almost everybody's life. So was humour. Of course we were all sinners so there was a lot to laugh about. While racism wasn't really that funny to the blacks and sexism wasn't so amusing to women of any colour, religion promised to fix all that in the sweet bye and bye.

Blue Belle sulked because I hadn't invited her to see the movie too, and threw the pillows off her chaise lounge and deliberately upset her basket of lace-embroidered handkerchiefs. It would have been too awkward with her there. Not that anybody but I could have seen her, but like Bitch, she would have tried to influence my conversation around the video. When Marian and Justin had gone for a walk afterward I tapped on Blue Belle's arch-framed entranceway draped with blue gauzy curtains. She wouldn't answer but I promised her through the curtains that we would see another movie together soon, one I was sure she would like. She still didn't answer, but I heard her blowing her nose so I knew she had heard me.

When I first immigrated to Canada I missed seeing black faces. After all, half the population of southern Louisiana is black. I knew Blue Belle missed that, too. So after some consideration and wanting to cheer Blue Belle up as well as hear some real southern black gospel music when nobody else was around, I invited her to sit with me to view Tyler Perry's play on video entitled Madea Goes to Jail.

This play, not to be confused with a later movie version of the same name, delights me. In it, writer and director Tyler Perry, a young black man, dons an elder black woman's wig, an oversized stuffed grandma dress and proceeds to display a wildly exaggerated version of black matriarchal humour through outrageous story lines. And within these story lines are experiences told of black life that I recognize as authentic. Okay, so I am not black myself but I was raised cheek by jowl with black people and my father occasionally preached in black churches. I immediately recognize genuine accents, cadences, singing, and gestures in some of the characters in this play. Rhodes found the video for me somewhere in Vancouver. He thought I might like it. I've watched it several times but this is the first time I've invited Blue Belle. I hesitated to even ask as I haven't wanted to set her off.

I have been somewhat worried about Blue Belle. She has been showing signs of depression. However, she seemed to perk up with my invitation. When I told her to come along as it was time for the video she smiled and hurriedly picked her nicest pink and blue hanky from her handkerchief basket. My sins were obviously forgiven. At least for the moment.

CHAPTER FIVE
Boy Children and Grown up Men

ALTHOUGH I KNEW BLUE BELLE WOULD RELATE VERY favourably to "Madea Goes to Jail" in terms of our shared southern culture, I wasn't sure how she would react to some of the more violent scenes. The violence concerned the sixteen-year-old daughter of a prisoner Madea had met in jail, who Madea had taken in after her release. The girl was a mess, so smart alecky the viewer just wanted to get up and slap her on screen. But she made the mistake of sassing Madea. Madea played a game she called "bottoms up" with the smart-mouthed out-of-control girl which amounted to a serious strapping with a belt. Across the mouthy teenager's bottom. But Blue Belle didn't flinch.

"No, I don't have any problem with that," Blue Belle said when I brought up my misgivings about what her reaction might be after the film ended. "You know what the Bible says about sparing the rod and spoiling the child." I nodded. But not in total agreement. Sure, in my time spankings and even strappings of unruly kids, mostly boys, were not unfamiliar, but, well...I'm sorry now I ever strapped my boys. I only did it twice with the two oldest ones. I was a very young single mother at my wits' end trying to stop little brotherly arguments that escalated from verbal insults to shoving then to hitting. But the time a brotherly argument ended in a trip to the hospital emergency ward is the one that stands out in my mind.

It was in 1956 in Phoenix, Arizona. We lived on the south side of the city, which meant, almost by definition, that we were too poor to buy health insurance. Had I been on welfare we would have fared somewhat better in the health care department but we weren't on welfare. As my ex-husband had remarried and contributed nothing in the way of child support, I supported my entire little family of three boys by working as a waitress in The Adams Hotel Restaurant in downtown Phoenix. While I was too poor to buy health insurance, I did have a cheap health care policy on all of us that provided six emergency visits each a year and a few days of hospitalization for each.

So the boys and I had health care via the emergency room, which remains the stupidest way imaginable to provide health care to the working poor, a policy that still exists in many parts of the States today. I'm Canadian now, and so are my boys but there were times back in Arizona when I wasn't sure we would ever get out of the neighbourhood, never mind the country. We had managed to stay even with our emergency room quota until the day ten-year-old Mike got into an altercation with his eleven-year-old brother Joey, and had to be taken to the emergency room.

It was a Friday afternoon. Our special family day. Every other Friday it was my turn at work to go home early from the restaurant. That day I had already arrived home and collected six-year-old Andy from Angela, the high school girl who conveniently lived next door. Angela escorted Andy to and from school as his first grade class started and ended earlier than the older boys' classes, and then Angela stayed with them all until I got home from work half an hour later.

However, on this day, one of our special afternoon days, Joey and Mike were late coming home from school. This had not happened before. Andy and I had made everything ready for a trip to Encanto Park: a picnic lunch, swim suits, towels. Encanto was a family park located in the centre of the city. It wasn't grand, but it was safe and had all the park necessities in a hotter than Hades place like Phoenix...a swimming pool, picnic tables, basket and volley ball courts, lots of green grass and little foot powered boats that kids could pump down a narrow, artificial stream.

We all loved the park - and it was cheap. A dime apiece for the boys to swim, a quarter for me, a dollar for all of us on the paddle boats. The boys always hurried home on my early afternoons off. But by four this Friday they hadn't returned. Had they been kept in detention? But that had never happened before. And they were in different grades. Seriously worried, I took Andy by the hand and headed toward the school to look for my two older sons.

We had just crossed the street when Joey and Mike appeared at the end of the block. Trouble. I could tell by the way they were yelling at each other. I stopped, waiting for them. As they came closer I saw they were bedraggled. They had been fighting. They could tell I was furious with them and walked silently behind me until we got into the house. Dreading the worst, I quickly inspected the boys for damage. Joey had a large puffed purpling bruise under his right eye but it was on his cheekbone, well under the eye socket. Mike's shirt was ripped open and bloodied. I didn't care about the shirt. But his mouth scared me. He was bleeding from his upper lip which was rapidly swelling. Teeth. Had his teeth been damaged? Very important, teeth. Cut and bruised flesh would heal without necessarily seeing a doctor. Broken teeth would require a dentist. After a hurried examination and in spite of Mike's yells that I was hurting him I could tell no teeth were broken. Then I corralled them both into the bathroom for a wash up and to see if I had missed anything. But no, just cuts and bruises. Relieved, I demanded an immediate explanation. This was a mistake; tempers were still smoldering.

"It was Mike's fault," Joey said heatedly, and then stalked out of the bathroom. Mike followed.

"It was not!" Mike yelled at Joey's retreating figure. I hurried after, trying to regain control of the situation.

Joey halted abruptly and faced his brother. "It was, too, and you know it!" he yelled at the same volume Mike was using. This was unusual for Joey. He had a peaceful nature and not only hated fights, but hated yelling. "You crossed the street and started fighting those Mexican kids first..."

"They were cussing at us..." Mike flung back, kicking off his runners and tugging fiercely at his bloodied shirt.

"And I told you not to listen," Joey retorted, almost screaming, as he advanced toward his brother.

Andy was taking all this in through big brown eyes. When Joey and Andy got into a serious tussle, perhaps because it happened so seldom, Andy appeared to doubt the stability of his universe. He started crying. And Andy had a mighty big cry for a little boy. I tried to soothe him, but he was inconsolable so I turned back to the other two.

"Okay, that's enough!" I yelled over the increasing din. "Mike, get those clothes off and everybody just calm down!"

Too late. Fuses had blown. As they had been threatening to since arriving home. Because Joey hated violence he had learned how to avoid fights. And while Mike didn't always start fights deliberately, he couldn't seem to walk away from them either. This was the second time in just a few weeks that Mike had dragged Joey into a real physical brawl and there had been other incidents where Joey had managed to pull Mike away from challenges. But only barely. Now Joey had had enough. And Mike wouldn't shut his still bloody mouth. He accused Joey of being a sissy. Joey took serious umbrage at that. He called Mike a dumb jackass at which point Mike, now wiping away bitter tears shoved Joey hard against the wall.

Joey flew at Mike, fists at the ready, and then the two were a tangle of flying fists and twisting medium sized boy bodies. They were evenly matched. While Joey was taller, Mike was stronger through the shoulders. And although they were both on the skinny side they were sturdy and strong and almost as tall as me. I couldn't separate them, so I went for the broom. That had worked before. And at first it seemed to be working again. By sticking the straw bottom of the broom between their flying fists the entire struggle got confused and amidst Andy's howling I managed to shove the tangled up boys out the front door and onto the front porch. In the past, they had stopped fighting almost immediately when people in the street laughed at them and made cat calls. But this time it didn't get to that stage. As soon as they hit the porch Joey landed a blow on Mike's shoulder that sent him reeling down the side of the steps feet first into a cholla cactus.

Cholla is murderous. Its little rounded green lobes look innocent enough but its thorns have tiny wicked hinges that go to work as soon as flesh is penetrated and swing open like winged screws. These thorns can kill small animals and makes penetrated human flesh a matter for surgery. Mike's shoeless left bare foot took the full impact of his fall into the cholla. His howls of pain brought Jive, Angela's dog, who also lived next door, running. Jive sailed over his six foot fence like an Olympic high jumper.

Jive was both a blessing and a curse. He actually belonged to Angela's father who was an ex-military man. The dog was some kind of a German Shepherd. Ex-police dog. Huge. He was not on friendly terms with the mailman. Or any strange man who tried to trespass on his territory. The boys and I had all been terrified of Jive when we first met him. But as Angela and her parents immediately became part of our lives, so did Jive.

This meant that his protected territory expanded to include our house and yard, too. This was okay with me. I didn't have to worry so much about intruders, especially at night.

But Mike and Andy's howling confused Jive and he just sat back on his haunches and started howling, too. Angela the baby sitter came running.

"What happened?" she asked anxiously. But at least Jive shut up and ran up to his household mistress, obviously glad to have somebody in charge enter the scene. Andy hushed and went to Angela. I explained that I had to take Mike to the hospital. Could she stay?

She could. As I went back into the house to get my purse I paused and patted Joey's shoulder. His big dark eyes were full of anxiety as they searched my face.

"It's not your fault," I said. "I don't blame you. Don't worry. And put some ice on your cheek while we're gone."

The anxiety in his eyes dissolved. "Do you want me to start some dinner?"

"Yes, that would be very good. Do the children's chili recipe. You know where the ingredients are. And I'll bring some ice cream on my way home."

He nodded and went back into the house followed by Angela and Andy. Mike and I sped off in my three hundred dollar Chevrolet coupe toward the hospital.

"I don't want to go to the hospital!" Mike cried as we headed up the boulevard. "I can take the thorns out. We don't have to go to the hospital!"

I ignored him. His bare foot was peppered with at least a dozen thorns, dug in deep in both the sole and his toes. When we arrived at the hospital Mike was so panicky at the thought of needles and things I had to go in and send an orderly out after him. With a wheelchair. This further humiliated Mike. Never mind, I told him firmly, this has to be done. And soon enough Mike was in a treatment room with a doctor and a nurse, while I sat just outside the door, limp with relief that he was in professional hands.

But not for long. Evidently, when Mike saw the needle being prepared for a local anesthetic for his foot he began to protest in earnest.

"No, don't stick me with that, I have to talk to my mother first," I could hear. "She doesn't know you're going to stick me with that."

"Yes, your mama knows," the doctor said in a thick, somewhat broken accent. This was an emergency room that routinely saw bullet-ridden bodies, stabbings, and blunt object trauma, the results of drunken driving, wife battering, and child neglect. "It will sting. Only for a moment," the doctor went on. "Be a man and hold still."

Instead, Mike hopped down off the table altogether and headed out the door, hobbling, but making strides. In fact, he was making tracks so fast he didn't even see me sitting by the door.

"I have to talk to my mother!" he yelled as he booted down the hall. I stared after him, momentarily struck dumb by this unexpected development. The boy was acting like he didn't have a lick of sense. The doctor and nurse spilled out of the treatment room in hot pursuit. I got up and joined the chase. But even with only one good foot, Mike was outrunning us all, and it wasn't until two nurses rounding the corner headed in our direction that there was a solution to the problem.

"Grab him!" the doctor yelled at the startled nurses. They galvanized into action and held my struggling son until the doctor could physically pick Mike up in his arms and cart him back to the treatment room. This time the doctor and three nurses held my son until the local anesthetic took hold and Mike quieted. When he emerged twenty minutes later, pale and shaken, his foot was swathed in bandages.

Mike was quiet on the way home, sobered by the ordeal. So was I. The clerk at the hospital had informed me that our emergency visit quota had indeed already been reached. Mike's adventure with the cactus had just cost us a whole week's wages. And it was my wages we were saving in the bank to try to buy a house.

The Adams Hotel where I worked was a first class hotel, the best in town at that time. Movie stars stayed there, as did professional ball players and many different kinds of famous people. One early afternoon in the dining room I even waited on Eleanor Roosevelt. At least I greeted her and escorted her to a table. That day the regular hostess was ill and I was asked to act as hostess in her place. I agreed reluctantly. While it was a chance to wear a nice dress instead of the waitress' rather gaudy tangerine coloured uniform, the higher salary I would get for the day wouldn't make up for the tips I would lose. However, the day's lost tips went right out of my head when I recognized Eleanor Roosevelt standing in the dining room doorway.

My knees went a little weak. Eleanor Roosevelt was just such an important person in the life of the nation. She was either revered or reviled. Her late husband, President Franklin D. Roosevelt, was mostly revered in the south, but not his wife. Not Eleanor. The First Lady was mostly reviled in the racist deep south, at least among white men. She had done the unthinkable. She had come out full strong for equality for black people and was instrumental in supporting the NAACP (The National Association for the Advancement of Colored People). So Eleanor Roosevelt was despised by southern men because number one, she wasn't pretty, and number two, she dared challenge the racist, male-dominated political structure of the south. But I loved her as did numbers of other southern women because she also went to bat for women.

In my job I had gotten used to serving movie stars such as Charlton Heston, Terry Moore, and Western movie stars like Gene Autry. The area around Phoenix was perfect for making Western movies. A lot of important conventions were held in the hotel, too, doctors and lawyers and international trade associations were frequent guests. And a half dozen or more of the New York Giants who were training in Phoenix gave me a baseball one morning after their breakfast and autographed the ball at their table. I thought the famous people were fun but they didn't awe me. Eleanor Roosevelt awed me. She had stood up to the racism in the south and this had helped black people and hadn't hurt her husband a bit. President Roosevelt is reported to have replied when questioned by reporters on his wife's activities, "Well, try as I might, I just cannot do a thing with Eleanor. You'll have to ask her those questions."

Of course the President could have done a lot about Eleanor's activities but he chose not to. And a significant number of women in the deep south, both black and white, stood up and cheered.

So I swallowed hard, pasted a bright smile on my face and welcomed the widow of the most famous man in the world, the most loved leader of all time, to our dining room. Wonderful. There was a table by the window that was free. Still shaky in the knees, I seated Mrs. Roosevelt, placed the menu before her and then opened it, hoping she wouldn't notice my trembling fingers. While she considered the menu I brought a glass of iced water with a slice of lemon to the table and informed her that her waitress would be right with her. Word had spread. I almost stumbled over Lena, who in her eagerness to make sure she was Mrs. Roosevelt's waitress, was breathing down my neck.

Other customers had appeared in the dining room doorway, a rather large party, so I walked away. What was the use of trying to make excuses to hang around Mrs. Roosevelt's table, I asked myself. Still, I might have had a chance to say something personal, like how much I admired her, how much my father loved her late husband, what a strong person I thought she was. But it would not have been appropriate. The hotel dining room was very firm in its rule that staff were not to initiate conversation with the guests. And I needed my job.

Twelve to fifteen dollars a day in tips doesn't sound like much now, but back then it was big. We lived on my tips from day to day; groceries, gas, and babysitting. I even paid our forty five dollars a month house rent from tips. Every evening after dinner, wash up and homework, Mike and Joey would count the day's tip money and make a note of it for deposit in the bank the next day.

A certain amount of the tip money was set aside for the drive in movie which could be had for a dollar a car load of kids, trips to the park, and treats. This amount went into a little ceramic pot we called our Jingle Pot. But my wage cheques went into the bank in a separate account to buy a house that was to be our ticket out of the worst part of the south side. And it was out of this fund that I would have to pay for Mike's foot.

"Did it cost a lot of money?" Mike asked as we turned down our street.

"Yes," I said. "A week's wages. It will have to come out of our housing fund."

He hung his head, his expression pensive. I knew he felt bad about this. The boys wanted a new house, too. And there was more than just talk of some low income houses being included in a new development just breaking ground on Buckeye Road. I had already talked to the management of the development who had given me an application to fill out for one of the low income houses.

"It's your temper, Mike," I admonished. "You have to learn to control it."

He fingered his shirt front. There hadn't been time to change the shirt during the melee. The front was open, buttons hanging or missing, and encrusted with dried blood. But Mike's upper lip was mostly swollen on just one side now. The doctor said it didn't need a stitch. Much to everybody's relief.

Mike looked over at me. "Mother, you don't control your temper some-times," he said defensively.

"What?" I asked sharply. I'd had about enough of this boy's sassiness for one day.

"I heard what you said to that guy who called you last night trying to get you to go out with him and you told him to go..."

"Hush," I broke in. "That's not your business and don't eavesdrop on my telephone calls. When there's something like that I want you to know I'll tell you about it."

He gave me a sour face. A sour face with a twisted swollen lip is not a pretty sight. But he didn't sass me. So when I stopped for ice cream at the corner store I thought what the hell and also bought chocolate sauce and frozen strawberries to go on top. Angela stayed for the ice cream and by the time it was all gone we were laughing at Jive who, still distressed by all the commotion and unable to find an enemy, just sat down on the kitchen floor and whined. He was eventually soothed by a few tablespoons of ice cream in a bowl.

Many years later, in conversation with Joey when he was in his thirties, we talked about those days when we were in between my marriages and we were so poverty stricken. I apologized to Joey for my strictness during his childhood, justifying it by saying I was very young myself and always worried that I couldn't keep the family together. He denied that his child-hood was unhappy, or even especially difficult. I accused him of being in denial. He denied being in denial. He asserted firmly that of all the guys he got to know well in the Air Force and later in his job as electrical engineer he thought his childhood was probably the happiest. And the one thing Joey said in that conversation that warms my heart even now: "Mother, in spite of everything we knew you loved us and that you would never leave us. That's what makes kids happy. All the other stuff is either immaterial or just...icing on the cake." I still think he may have been fudging a little bit but he is gone now and I'm glad we had that conversation.

No, I didn't leave my son. But he left me some fifteen years after that conversation, via the cancer train that crosses this continent on a daily run gathering up passengers by the thousands. And I'm not alone. I'm not the only mother left behind when I should have boarded that train before my children. And I will never forgive the governments and corporations and the oh-so-learned doctors and cancer researchers who dump this devastating disease back on the afflicted instead of demanding that serious money and attention go into researching pollutants that are causing the cancer epidemic.

The video of the play Madea Goes to Jail came to a rousing close culminating with the mother of the sixteen year old girl released from jail and returning to the reluctant arms of her now reformed daughter (reformed by Madea's tough love campaign) and singing in true gospel style. All the music in the play was true gospel style (that is, the style Blue Belle and I know best). At the close Blue Belle was weeping a little.

"Oh, I loved it," she sighed, wiping her moist cheeks with one of her dainty handkerchiefs. "How everything turned out all right with everybody loving and trusting and turning their hearts over to God."

I gave a little only half-concealed snort. Blue Belle glared at me through still reddened eyes. "Oh, make fun. Go ahead and make fun. But the reason you find this film so entertaining is because you know there's a lot of truth in it."

"All right, Blue Belle, but it's because there is some truth in most religions, even aboriginal ones, isn't that so?"

"Perhaps. But you're not Indian and God didn't sit you down in a Muslim or Buddhist country now, did He? He put you right here in a God fearing Christian country..."

"Blue Belle, we're not in Louisiana now. We're in Canada."

"Well, Canada is primarily Christian, too..."

"I'm not so sure about that," I said, remembering a news report. "At least in British Columbia. I heard somewhere not long ago that English has slipped to second place as the predominant language spoken in BC. Or maybe it was in the Vancouver area. Whatever, this end of the country is certainly being saturated with Muslims and Hindus along with Buddhists and other people who are not Christian."

Her eyes widen. "Really? But that's awful!"

"Please, Blue Belle, don't make me embarrassed that I even know you. All patriarchal religions are the same. Their primary purpose is to subjugate women and aggrandize men. It doesn't matter a helluva whole lot..."

"Yes, it does, you know it does," she snapped, slipping into in her flashing blue eyed argumentative best. "Christian women don't have to go around wearing scarves on their heads all the time, we Christian women can show our hair to the world and we can go out of the house whenever we want without asking our husbands or for Pete's sake, our sons...and watch your language. Ladies don't swear."

She was wound up. And I wanted to go to bed. I bade her a hasty good night and escaped. But once in bed I couldn't sleep. I shouldn't have watched the Madea film, I thought. Watching that film and others made by Tyler Perry which feature black people searching for and eventually finding God in extremely difficult circumstances, portrayed in broad, slapstick humour, a particular kind of black humour that tickles many white southerners although Perry's core following is black, made me home sick. Not so much for country anymore, because I know the particular part of the country that I long for from time to time has been irrevocably destroyed; the Louisiana wetlands as I knew them, where I knew them, were gone.

But the language in the film, the language was so familiar to me, and yet it's almost like another language altogether. When I have tried to interest friends and family members in Perry's films they are either shocked by the humour or just don't get it. All have more than a little difficulty understanding what the actors are saying because the accents are so thick and the references so foreign to them.

But perhaps the films weren't good for me, either. They tugged at my heart strings. I wallowed in the joy of their singing, real black gospel singing, and in the belief that in the end God would make things right.

And I knew that wasn't so. There was no God up there or anywhere, God is us. The idea of God is us. In my opinion as long as I, or anybody else, wherever they may hang out, in whatever language or custom, hang on to the concept that God is somewhere outside us then there can't be any real evolutionary progress for humans.

Yes, of course we humans need to celebrate the mysteries of life. We need to find times to humbly acknowledge our connections with all other forms of life, to search the past for the voices that have proven wise, not to worship, but to gather into our own beings the words and deeds that have represented the journeys of the many who came before us, of those humans who sought to further the process of evolution not just in humans, but in all of our relations and to look forward with confidence...but to what?

Funny, as I tried to understand my struggle with ole time religion that night after watching Madea Goes to Jail and the exchange with Blue Belle, I thought about when I was first in prison and heard this line from a First Nations prayer, "and for all of our relations," at the end of a "smudge." A smudge is a cleansing prayer done with sweet grass smoke, and at first I thought the reference "for all our relations" was to remember actual relatives. But it isn't. The prayer refers to all of the earth's wild creatures who haven't the voice to call to the Creator for cleansing. Assuming the animals felt they needed cleansing. How could they even feel such a thing? Did humans feel the need for cleansing back in Neanderthal Days when we were hardly removed from the other animals ourselves? Of course not. Humans couldn't feel that need until they became aware of sin. But I was assured by the Elder that the prayer also asks that the supplicants' hands, feet, and hearts be set on a good path. So different from my own memories of searching for the spiritual... Gimme that ole time religion...it's good enough for me...

But it wasn't. Not for me. Not anymore. I valued my mind above all. I was at my most moral, most elevated, most in tune with myself and the universe when I tried to learn, to understand, to make connections between what I knew and what I thought I needed to know. And yes, the old time gospel music tugged at my heart but in the same way a sentimental movie does; at some important level I was always conscious of manipulation. But what I had learned from my self-directed studies was mine; I broke these studies apart and let them seep into my bones, be absorbed into my blood stream through my endocrine system; all fed my brain. And while I was not sure what good this did me, or anybody in the long run, it helped me live and once in a while to feel a deep, resounding joy.

When I wake the morning after the Madea film I realize I have to start making some additional, more expansive plans for summer visitors. Marian's father will be coming for a visit on the 21st, leaving around the 31st. Wally and I divorced many years ago. Marian is his only child although he acted as stepfather to all my daughters for half a dozen years or so when they were very young. As he and I are not good friends (or really friends at all), I'll take this time to visit daughters Rose Mary and Margaret Elizabeth and their husbands and children in Ucluelet while Wally visits. Actually, only Rose Mary has children, three to be exact, the eldest married and living in Vancouver, the two younger ones in their teens and still in the nest. Rose Mary's house stays busy. Besides the teenage girls and husband Jim, a dog, a cat, two birds and several dozen fish live there. And guppies, I remember. Margaret's household includes husband Andre, and a large, beautiful, arrogant cat named Kitty Brown along with two young wild deer who don't exactly live in the house but eat their way around it several times a day and fascinate Kitty Brown no end.

Many benefits will accrue from absenting myself from the house while Marian's father is visiting. Just about everything either of us says annoys the hell out of the other. By going visiting I won't toy with high blood pressure and Marian won't have to skirt around ten tension-filled days and can enjoy her father's company in peace. And I could use some peace myself. The house has been full of people and I have a personality that enjoys periods of reserve mixed with a lot of gregariousness; I feel a reserved period coming on.

Rhodes is in Vancouver helping Laird. Laird is my son-in-law, married to my oldest daughter, Susan. He installs industrial doors. I miss Rhodes. He is my guy Friday. But I want to think, really think about the book Marian and Justin gave me for my birthday. It's called War and Sex. And I know I can depend on Bitch to bring to my attention anything she considers important in the book that she thinks I might overlook.

War and Sex turns out to be wonderfully insightful and informative, especially considering that it was largely written by two men, Dr. Malcolm Potts and Mr. Thomas Hayden. Potts, the main voice, does give credit to his wife for two of the chapters but it's still a man's book, written for men, I think. It's unique nevertheless, one of the few I've read written by the male sex that is truly friendly to women. The authors' main premise is that biology is, in a very real sense, destiny. Usually, this term is applied in reference to women, and used to keep women in their supposed proper places, but these authors talk about men and how their predisposition for violence, both physically and mentally, is bringing us to the edges of earth collapse. And how men have to come to grips with this tendency or we're all in danger of falling off the edges.

The authors get down and dirty when talking about men's predisposition to gather into small male groups, which evolve into small enclaves, or in-groups, which lead to the formation of larger groups, eventually becoming one collective group which then perceives other groups of men as out-groups. All of the groups vie for resources and control over females and reproduction, and territory. Thus hostilities develop. The out-groups of course consider themselves to be in-groups and the other in-groups, as out-groups. Got that? And when male out-groups and in-groups affiliate into ever-larger groups the tendency of all of them is to consider other groups as less human. Enter gang wars, rebellions, uprisings, all-out war. And we have rape.

Conflict rape has been classified a war crime by the UN. Few care. At least it seems so. Except of course the women being raped and their immediate families who may disown them entirely if the women are unfortunate enough to live in a part of the world where men are fighting over resources and the right to control women absolutely. In such places women will be blamed for being raped because they are, in essence, inferior beings who are capable of being raped, and therefore must be punished severely (if not outright killed) for their crime of being women caught in men's war games.

So I thank Potts and Hayden for making an insightful contribution to the evolution of the human race by bringing their perspectives to the fore in scientific terms. More or less. And oh yes, these two writers and researchers also consider male emotional development to be really not far removed from that of chimpanzees. Thank heavens; I thought I was the only one giving this perception serious consideration. But I think the good authors have overlooked something. Something important which they touch on, but do not elaborate on, in this book. I want to pursue this so I will take the book with me on my visit to my families in Ucluelet.

In hindsight it was a very wise choice to clear the home premises while Marian's father visited. I love schmoozing (and yes, sometimes fighting) with my offspring, especially if I haven't seen them in months, which was the case with Margaret Elizabeth and Rose Mary when I arrived in Ucluelet. I had a lovely time with them and my granddaughters. And my sons-in-law, although sometimes we tread gingerly around each other. Matriarch. That's what I am. Sometimes I revel in it.

Things went well with Wally's visit. During the second week of his visit Wally even came to Ucluelet with Marian and two of his friends on the little cruise ship Mary Rose (not to be confused with my daughter Rose Mary) from Nanaimo to have lunch with his ex-step-daughters and to meet his ex-step-daughter's children. Rose Mary and Margaret pulled off a tight time line. Rose Mary made reservations at Black Rock, a new resort with a large patio that faces the sea and serves great salmon and promised to have everything ready so our guests could be served and driven back to the ship in time for departure. Margaret Elizabeth left work early to help her sister greet their guests and help ferry everybody to and fro. Cars, food, conversation, weather, scenery, all conspired to make the lunch a huge success. And I even enjoyed it.

I hadn't seen Wally in five years, and it had been much longer since Margaret Elizabeth and Rose Mary had seen their ex-step father who had played an important role in their early years. It could all have been very awkward but too many people were having a good time and I didn't have a chance to exchange thinly disguised verbal barbs with Wally even had I been so inclined. Which I wasn't. And the girls were simply delighted to see him again.

But there was no time during my visit to the West Coast to ponder the information I was gleaning from War and Sex. I was too busy reconnecting with my living relatives. And my dead ones.

The ashes of my dead ones are scattered in an inlet off the West Coast Trail in Ucluelet. Joey, my first born. Fifty-seven. Cancer. In his brain. Later, everywhere. Barbara Ellen, my seventh child. She was thirty when she died. Breast cancer. After Wally and his friends sailed away on the Mary Rose Margaret Elizabeth and I visited the bench dedicated to Barbara Ellen. The bench presides over a little outcropping facing the sea that is now part of the West Coast Trail. The point where my children's ashes were scattered into the sea is just around the bend. While the bench does not overlook that particular point the view is incredible. Margaret and I sat and contemplated the nature of the universe while watching the sea. The everlasting sea. I came home much refreshed.

August is now over. Marian left yesterday, the third of September. Rhodes is still working in Vancouver. I have the entire place to myself as I have resisted all efforts on Marian's part to try to arrange for someone to stay with me until she returns. I don't need a baby sitter. Not yet. And I like being alone. Except I'm not really alone as I am increasingly pestered by Blue Belle and Bitch. And as I am presently less distracted by having hordes of people about, Bitch wastes no time in coming on strong, guns blazing, blood in her eyes.

CHAPTER SIX
Find Stockholm Syndrome

"DID YOU HEAR, DID YOU HEAR?" BITCH DEMANDS JUST AS I sit down in the early morning to my computer. She leans against my desk as if she belongs there. This office came equipped with one of those corner office desk arrangements that features two rather large, distinct working areas bound on each end by individual book cases. As it has a kind of built in look, the previous owners just left the arrangement here when they moved out. Marian and I share this office space, but when she is away I fall prey to sideways sprawl and my books and papers soon also grace her desk space.

"What?" I ask guardedly. "Have women taken over the world?"

She chortles with glee. I hate Bitch's chortle. There is something vicious in it.

"Not the world. Maybe just Canada."

"I see. On what do you base this startling turn of events?"

"The work force. It was on the news early this morning after you drifted back to sleep."

I feel a twinge of anger. Maybe just anxiety. "I don't like you coming into my room when I'm asleep," I say sharply.

"Oh, for God's sake," she counters. "Half the time you're asleep when you're awake, anyway. How would I know?"

I glare at her. She smirks.

"I have to get to work," I snap. "Do you mind?"

"You don't even want to know what I heard about the work force."

"Okay, tell me. Get on with it. What about the work force that has you so excited?"

"Well...since you asked...there are now as of the first six months of the year more women in the work force in Canada than men."

I give a start. Is this true? And what would that mean?

"Fine. Now go away," I say after a moment, not wanting to invite conversation on the matter even if it proves to be true. As soon as Bitch ungraciously vacates my office I Google "Canadian women in the work force." It's true. Bitch heard right. More Canadian women than men were in paid employment during the first half of 2009, according to Statistics Canada. But perhaps this doesn't mean much, I think.

Women still earn on average 71.4% of what men earn for similar hours. Women haven't really made any gains; it's just that men have lost jobs in male-dominated sectors because of the recession. Poor Bitch. She wants women to be the leaders of society so desperately she will try to spin any morsel of news that can be spun in that direction. No, no cause for celebration in this announcement. Except that women endure. More women are picking up the mantle of multiple jobs and tasks in the face of a failing economy. And enduring. But I have to get back to War and Sex. And the important issue the authors touched upon but then shied away from like a swamp mule confronting a nest of rattlesnakes.

According to Potts and Hayden, it's all about the in-groups and out-groups that men form that link us all to the chimpanzees. Women have empathy for each other but don't form the same kind of in-group, out-group relationships that men do, which can readily turn out-groups of people into something less than human. But once physical fighting starts women can be as fearless as men. We are told about the border fighting between Ethiopia and Eritrea and the fearlessness of the Eritrean female fighters. We are told two different things about these Eritrean women soldiers: that they were ruthless with male prisoners, preferring to kill them rather than take them prisoner, but that they did take steps to try to protect the women on the opposing side (we are not told what steps these were). Potts and Hayden continue:

> During the Liberian civil war in 2001 and 2002, a young
> woman who called herself "Colonel Black Diamond"

controlled an all-woman troop of fighters. She carried a pistol and a cell phone and wore tight-fitting jeans, an embroidered strapless top, pink nail polish, and a red bandana. Black Diamond and most of the other women in her troop had been raped during the course of the war. Perhaps not surprisingly, the women had formed an in-group of their own. It seems possible that women as fighters are more focused on defense and survival than are men. That is what we would expect if they do indeed lack the male genetic predisposition to band together as we saw in the previous chapter, (and will) occasionally empathize and fraternize with the enemy - so long as there is an implicit in-group connection.

An in-group connection was recognized and acted upon by the women warriors of Black Diamond's army, who occasionally empathized and fraternized with the enemy, as long as the enemy soldiers were other females. The connection? Aside from just being the same sex? All of the women lived in intensely patriarchal societies.

Potts and Hayden go on to say that most of the women soldiers had undergone female genital mutilation..."a painful experience that might have helped cement a bond similar to that shared by Black Diamond and her cohorts."

But for me, an almost throw-away sentence by Potts and Hayden is the most telling, the one observation about these women fighters that made bells and whistles ring in my head: "Perhaps for Black Diamond and her troop, and the Ethiopian women as well, men on the whole are actually an out-group."

You think? That some women could view all men as an out-group? After being raped how many times by how many soldiers? And were some of the rapes friendly fire? That is, by soldiers on their own side. As happens today with female soldiers in the US army. And female genital mutilation. As little girls. With the entire clitoris and other body parts cut out and tender bleeding flesh sewn back up with infection-laden knives and needles. A procedure that not only can make future child bearing painful but dangerous beyond imagination. Without anesthesia or means to stop possible hemorrhaging and with no possibility of ever enjoying normal sex or experiencing orgasm...

Yes. My gut reaction, without any urging at all from Bitch, is yes; I can definitely see how these women soldiers could come to see all men on all sides of the conflict as out-groups, even their own side. But most men regardless of where they are or what they do, don't want to hear this kind of thing. And why would they? To them it sounds like man hating. Their heads could never wrap around the notion that there should ever be any reason, however heinous, for women to consider men as an out-group. Aren't men the protectors of women, for Pete's sake?

I'm alone in the house in Merryland, have been for weeks. After five years of intense activity punctuated primarily by grief for the deaths of my son and my daughter, prison sentences and court appearances, all of these generating interactions with many people, I am happy to be alone for a while. It is well into September now and our beautiful garden is showing signs of fading. I am still eating tomatoes from the green house, though, and onions. And blackberries. So many blackberries from the one big bush on the side of the house. I am tired of eating them and have sugared and frozen some just as Marian treated the sweet little peaches from our peach tree before she left. But the over ripe cherries are still dropping from the inaccessible (at least to me) branches at the top of the cherry tree and are making a mess on the ground and walkway.

Next year I will call in time for volunteers who will come and pick fruit for the food bank. What a good idea. However, there is no time to luxuriate in the bounty of the earth. Yesterday was the day of 9/11 remembrances. And they are, of course, still on the radio today.

I have an innate predisposition for conspiracy theories. But even bearing my penchant in mind, I cannot believe that the serial assassinations of leaders in my life time in the US were random acts of violence by individual men, that is, that the murders of Malcolm X, John Kennedy, Robert Kennedy, and Martin Luther King were all unrelated and all done by individual screwballs. And I'm beginning to believe that there was something incredibly fishy about 9/11.

The fishiest thing about 9/11 is this: how did these two hijacked planes get past the Air Force that was supposed to be guarding the most important air space in America? The Twin Towers of world finance? The Pentagon?

Well, we're told that the US Air Force was too busy at the time, involved in doing air exercises at the very moments the twin towers were struck and that the exercise was, would you believe...practicing what to do in case terrorists invaded the air space around the most important targets of finance and the Pentagon. That the air force pilots were confused and thought the signals they were getting about hijacked planes were part of the exercise? Now I ask you...isn't that a bit much? Isn't that just a little too much of a coincidence? Too much of a stupid coincidence? If it is true, then the US government military forces are so stupid the US cannot possibly survive. I do not believe this is true. I think this explanation is a lie. However, the day's work is done and I'm ready to watch something light hearted and funny that has nothing to do with 9/11. I find another Madea DVD and take it upstairs to the TV room.

Actually, we are not wired for TV in this house. I have rarely been wired for TV in my lifetime. TV has always scared the hell out of me. But not movies. One can pick and choose what videos to watch. This one is called The Diary of a Mad Black Woman. As I start the movie Blue Belle appears in the doorway. Again, I have invited her. She takes a seat and I wait until she settles her flouncy skirt and then the movie begins.

What is so intriguing about this movie is that Tyler Perry plays Madea, the violent, rambunctious grandmother of the female lead in the movie, and also Daddy Charles, the aged father of the lead's husband who is a lawyer. The lawyer is rotten beyond belief. Daddy Charles is much like a male version of Madea except that he appears not to be so robust physically until the singing starts. There is one very funny long scene of singing and dancing and pot smoking, however, it is when he is playing Madea that Perry, in my opinion, approaches genius.

Why this should be so, I wonder, watching the film. Why should a young handsome black man who writes, produces, and stars in his own film seem rather stiff when playing a straight role, funny, when he is playing a dirty minded twisted old man, but absolutely hilarious when he plays an equally twisted old black woman who constantly flings cruel and crude remarks to the world at large and carries a handbag full of guns that shoot only blanks and yet who strives for justice? It is within the personality of Madea, the irreverent black grandmother, that this young screenwriter finds his true voice.

But is this character that lives in Perry's head similar to my own Bitch? Is that why I find Madea so funny? Because she is like Bitch? And is Perry's "Cora," the wonderful religious black singer who always plays the role of mother in his films, the one who leads the erring ones back to God, able to touch my heart with her role because she is like Blue Belle? And thus like my own mother, and even me when I was young?

Sorta. I guess. Somehow Tyler Perry manages to insert ancient archetypes into his characterizations so they are instantly recognizable, the good from the bad, and even the grey is nudged over to the Godly side unless the characters have consorted with the devil so long they are irredeemable. Like the father of the foster child in the play Madea Goes to Jail who looked for his sixteen year old daughter so he could prostitute her. And the singing. Oh my God, the singing. It's opera unlike any other. Blue Belle and I part on good terms, happy with the film's ending.

The morning dawns bright and beautiful and when I take my breakfast out on the deck I find Bitch waiting for me. She is sitting at the end of the deck table. She gives me a twisted little grimace of a smile as I plunk down my breakfast plate. The two poached eggs wobble slightly from the thrust and then settle. I take my chair and start eating. Bitch knows I am not happy to see her. She also knows that I know she is not happy with me. The Madea film. She doesn't like it when I watch this kind of film with Blue Belle.

Bitch is also from the south, but she's traveled all over the world. And even though she's from Louisiana, she wasn't raised in the country. She doesn't understand. She grew up on the streets of New Orleans. She gives me a brief, accusing glare and then drops her eyes. Her nails suddenly become the object of her attention. She pretends she is working on a hang nail, biting at the side of her scrawny forefinger. I ignore her, gazing out over the back yard as I eat. The yard is very pleasant. However the grass needs mowing again and the grapevine climbing up the post of the deck overhead should be restrained. I have decided that plants, particularly vines, are not as smart as they are sometimes touted by humans. According to my plant loving friends the ever growing tendrils of the grapevine I am studying at the moment should seek the stability of the post without my help, but no... the tendrils are waving wildly in the air away from the post, as if calling for help from any passerby. I will have to tie them to the post, for Pete's sake, in order to guide them to their destination. Like swaddling a baby.

The bees are already busy on the blackberry bush by the side of the house. I have just taken a bite of toast when I spot the lone, hesitant wasp circling my breakfast table in erratic, zigzag motions. I watch the flight path for a moment, waiting. The wasp's hesitance to light somewhere close to my plate comes, I am sure, from the adventure we shared the previous morning. Bold little bugger had decided to simply join me for breakfast by lighting on the edge of my plate. Actually, these little meetings had been going on for several weeks. I had originally taken the position that there was enough on my plate to share and anyway, the wasp usually lost its nerve before actually diving into my plate. But after a random, unprovoked attack on my head several days earlier, I had rethought the sharing thing. And after a trip to the dollar store in Courtenay for some fly swatters I felt better prepared to defend myself against unexpected preemptive strikes.

The previous morning the wasp had crossed boundaries. Not only had he buzzed around my head again but then immediately landed on my plate. I had smacked the creature a good one but as it had already snuggled deep into the fold of my scrambled egg it was only stunned. And its rapid recovery was marvelous to behold. In the blink of an eye it had staggered up, shaken off some residual scrambled egg, flown straight up into the air; and then zigzagging wildly, disappeared from sight. And here it is again. I sit, coffee cooling, waiting.

First, the wasp makes a couple of investigative sorties close to my head, darting swiftly in and out. I don't react. Unless it actually lands on my head, I know it's best not to move. Darting, then hovering, more darting, the little dance goes on for several moments. It finally comes to rest on the edge of the table, and just sits there for a moment, obviously unsure about advancing to my plate. My hand, ever so slowly, searches the seat of the chair next to mine where the fly swatter rests; my fingers close stealthily around the handle; I'm ready to call into action a simple but useful implement. Yes, be afraid, I mentally advise the wasp. Be very afraid. The wasp and I stare at each other. Fly swatter firmly in hand under the table, I don't move. Or blink. After a long moment, seemingly unnerved by the calm but determined stance of the opposition, the wasp apparently decides to hell with it, and takes off. It's too beautiful a morning to die for a nip of scrambled egg. Especially when the back yard is swarming with meaty little insects.

I finish my coffee leisurely, enjoying the morning. And trying not to look at Bitch. Sometimes if I refuse to acknowledge her she'll go away.

"You found Harriet Nahanee's paper on the Stockholm Syndrome, didn't you?" she asks after a moment. Her voice isn't accusing, exactly. Just matter of fact. I look at her. In the early morning bright light she is grotesque. Not that she isn't always more or less grotesque, but this morning she is scarier looking than usual. Several loose tendrils of multi-colored hair wave about her weathered, wrinkled face much like the grapevine tendrils searching for something, anything, to cling to that might be within reach. Her skirt is short, torn as if she simply ripped one of her longer ones, and the unevenly ripped hem rides high around her strong, skinny, mottled legs. No shoes. Funny toes. But it's her eyes that make me look away. The full force of the glaring morning sun has stirred up the depths of something in her eyes I don't want to see, some kind of passion that makes her enlarged pupils glitter like ice, like diamonds, like death. I turn my head.

"Yes, I found it," I admit. "So? And have you been smoking a joint?"

She doesn't answer. I squint against the sun, trying to stall Bitch. I do not want to get into a discussion about Harriet's paper. It's just too bloody hot. So early in the morning, too. And so late in the year. After all, we are already into October.

"Yes, I read it when Harriet first gave it to me," I reply finally. "I'm going inside. I'm getting a headache."

I left her sitting there. She didn't try to follow me and as the morning progressed I dismissed her from my mind. I had a full day of work before me and I also needed to talk to Rhodes about his revised plans. He was back from Vancouver after a falling out with his aunt's husband. But Bitch didn't let me go. Oh, no. She resurfaced later. Although she did let me finish the last episode of The Tudors on my little lap top in my bedroom that evening before she made her presence known.

CHAPTER SEVEN
Flack from Blue Belle

BITCH HAS SEATED HERSELF IN THE LITTLE GREEN BOUDOIR chair, a gift that's really too small to be comfortable for me, but which fits her skinny aged butt just fine. She is holding a copy of my latest blog entry entitled Bountiful and Bombings. In this piece I referred to the sect of Fundamentalist Church of Jesus Christ of Latter Day Saints who live in Bountiful, British Columbia. One of the churchmen recently charged is reported to have twenty-seven wives. The charges have been dropped against him and another Bountiful peach of a man with multiple wives on a technicality. Which is reluctance on the part of Crown prosecutors to argue the matter of illegality (really a kind of laziness and lack of political will): they cite fear of a Constitutional challenge regarding Freedom of Religion, never mind that this is supposed to be what law is about.

In my recent blog I compared the failure to bring a man with 27 wives to account for breaking the civil law in Canada with another bombing of a girl's elementary school in Pakistan on religious grounds. This group considers it un-Islamic for girls to be educated. If they can read and write there is a possibility they will rebel against burkas and stonings and such. It seems that the tie that binds all major world religions is the same one that binds all women to their twin yokes of sex and service. Nothing human here, you know, for woman, all animal stuff. I thought it a fairly good article. Missiles, I call them. But no, Bitch is frowning.

"So what?" I ask, exasperated. "Isn't it good enough for you?"

"It's okay," she answers handing the paper to me. "But look. You didn't define both of these conditions as being overt sexual slavery, which these practices are... sexual slavery that is made possible either by men's laws or just by men's customs."

"It's a blog," I answer sharply. "It's not a book."

"Yes, and leave her alone about it," a new voice demands. I give a little start but don't have to look around. I know who it is. Blue Belle. Like Bitch, she's taken to appearing unannounced.

"Betty is trying to present a more balanced picture than one your own ratty mind could possibly conceive," Blue Belle continues, managing her full skirt and petticoat with ease and grace as she makes a seat for herself at the foot of my bed.

"Ratty? You call my mind ratty?" Bitch asks. And then she laughs. It's a real laugh, not one of her scary chuckles, but she quickly composes herself. "You have a nerve, little girl. That's what you are, a little girl. You know nothing. Your head is stuffed full of myths and superstitions and you have a hangdog quality that wants a strong master. One that beats you, preferably."

Blue Belle stiffens. "That isn't true. I've never been beaten. I have always been careful to choose men who were...well, decent. Of course...on the rare occasion when my man...slapped me...I knew it was because I had done something to deeply displease him that I shouldn't have and I believe very strongly that a man should be the head of the house."

"Uh-huh. Only you're not in your man's house now. You're in Betty's head. Why don't you go back to your own house where your man can slap you around occasionally as you think you so richly deserve?"

Blue Belle slides gracefully off the edge of my bed. Her little chin is stuck out a mile and her lower lip is trembling but her voice is strong as she rises to Bitch's challenge.

"I won't leave Betty. If I left her you would take her over entirely. And that would be a terrible thing. Your way is the devil's way. Women weren't meant to rule men. The Bible says women were to be men's helpmates. What you want is unnatural. And that includes other unnatural things you think that are unspeakable..."

Bitch's eyes narrow and glitter. "So tell me, little girl, just what are these unnatural unspeakable things?"

"You know what they are! I don't have to spell them out for you, any of them, but they will all take you straight to hell and I'm not letting you lead Betty there, too! At least not without a struggle! She belongs to me! Her mother gave her to me and I want her in the service of the Lord, not to waste her talents on the likes of you and your evil ideas, but on the Lord's work, on glorifying God..."

Blue Belle pauses and takes a deep breath that ends with a hiccup. Bitch and I both stare at her.

"I'm going," she says and leaves, skirts flouncing. Bitch turns to me.

"You're going to have to kill her," she says slowly. "You will never get rid of her unless you kill her."

"Oh, stop it," I say. "On second thought, maybe I need to kill both of you."

Bitch uncoils slowly from the boudoir chair. "Okay, maybe I've pushed too soon. You're not ready for my message yet. I'll see you later. But just reread the first line of Harriet's version of the Stockholm Syndrome. Just the first line. And we'll talk about it, okay?"

She's gone. I lean back weakly on my pillow. These two exhaust me. The first line? Okay, I'll read the damn first line, just to get Bitch off my back. Because, yes, I've found the worrisome thing, but where did I put it? I get out of bed and scrabble through the various assorted mind-boggling, world-changing essays of mine and other peoples' that are in haphazard piles on my little bedroom desk and voilà, I find the troublesome thing that Bitch is trying to worry me to death over.

I take the single sheet of paper back to bed. As I ponder the first line I wonder if this is Harriet's handwriting. It's written in large bold black letters with scribbled x's and u's. More like a guy's handwriting, I think. And the text of the entire thing is very brief. Four, five lines max. But my assignment is just the first line. The heading is misspelled as "Stockholm Syndrom." But that doesn't matter: the first line reads: You are taken prisoner by terrorists.

Okay. Certainly other definitions I've Googled on the Stockholm Syndrome have less straightforward first lines. When Harriet had talked to me about the paper on the Eagleridge Bluffs blockade she had equated the Stockholm Syndrome to the capture of Indians on this continent by white people. Were the Indians taken prisoner? Yes, of course. Those the whites didn't kill. The Indians who survived were taken prisoner by white men (white women followed later, desperate women for the most part or they wouldn't have risked their lives to come to such a dangerous country to hook up with such dangerous men). Yes, even though the Indians were in their own land, they were taken prisoner and brutally driven onto reservations. Later, their children were sent to residential schools – "reform" schools in the most literal sense - where they were beaten and raped. Of course the Indians were prisoners. Then and now. Even if they are not required to stay on reservations at present, the free floating racism of white culture will get many of them willy-nilly, out of all proportion to their population, in spite of some outstanding successes. Prisoners? Yes. And most of the women I served time with in prison were native.

While I was incarcerated, many sister prisoners told me the prisons just take up where the residential schools left off. And family services, children's services, foster homes, meagre welfare, juvenile detention (juvie, they call it) demoralization and neglect set the course for much of the precious, loving, loved Indian life, life that inhabited the ancient native populations on contact, life that could have taught the whites many things, life that honoured women and took pride in caring for elders and communities, that shared...no, capitalism couldn't stand that.

If the Indian concept of communal and shared living with its respect for women had prevailed it would have nipped capitalism in the bud before it even got off the ground. I have always believed that the hatred shown native populations by whites, even now shown in this culture, had - and has - more to do with the spirit of community the Indians seemed imbued with, than it has with dislike for brown skins. The belief that everything must be shared and the biggest person is the biggest giver, not the biggest keeper. Scary business. This just didn't mesh with rugged individualism, the mantra of capitalism. Greed. Indians just didn't like greed and didn't want to consider this the big goal in life. So they drank, sniffed, injected, and killed themselves. The white culture didn't realize and still doesn't, in my opinion, that most of the Indian cultures on contact were profoundly good. Sweet and good. To care for the natural world. For children, all of the children in the community. Old people were the mainstay that held the world together. Respect was measured by what you did for the community as a whole.

Of course, pre-contact life on this continent wasn't perfect. There were warring tribes, losers were even sometimes taken as slaves, injustices were committed, but most Indian cultures defined a good person as someone

who served his or her people without expecting a reward. I found this wonderful when I first read about Indian culture, that there was no expectation
of material reward, only respect from the community. My God, this sounds
impossibly idealistic, yet before white contact it was the inner core of native
lives, of their stories, of their spiritual beliefs. So how could Indian nations
live under this paradigm when the whites were obviously superior because
they had guns?

They couldn't. Not without profound mental, spiritual, and economic
carnage which was what they got anyway. But many, maybe even most, truly
learned the white man's ways, how to disrespect women by treating them as
sex objects, by beating them, by refusing to care for them in any humane,
consistent way, and how to love money, goods, brute economic and armed
power in the process. But are women in general captive? Black, white,
Indian? Were they back then? Way back then?

Perhaps. It seems that women lost their right to be anything but captive
goods back then, back five thousand years ago, whatever they might have
been before the rise of patriarchy and the world religions. And if women
put up a fuss about being treated as captives, by the fall of the Roman
Empire they had forgotten about it. By then it was forget it or die. And the
witch burnings were still going on about the same time white men on this
continent were killing and raping the Indians and plundering their land.
So yes, I think we could say there was a kind of parallel in terrorist activities, in the capture and killing of all Indians that white men could safely get
at, and in tightening of the captivity of non-native women.

Okay, Bitch, I've passed the test for the first article of Harriet's Stockholm
Syndrome 101, I think. But I am not yet allowed to sleep. Blue Belle has
returned. She takes the seat across from my bed that Bitch recently vacated.

"I want to say a few words about this," she says, primly smoothing down
her fluffy skirt. I sigh and lay my papers on the side of the bed.

"Yes, Madame," I answer, giving her my full attention. I have learned
the hard way that if Blue Belle feels she has been heard she isn't inclined to
overstay her welcome.

"That is ridiculous and you know it," she continues, making rather
fierce eye contact.

"What?" I ask innocently. But I know what she is referring to. And she
knows I know.

"That sheet of paper Witch gave you. Women aren't captives. Neither are Indians. They are free to leave their reservations if they want to. And a lot have. I read where more Indians now are living off reservations than on. Isn't that freedom? To move wherever you want to?"

"Yes, Blue Belle, in the same way a rich man is just as free to live under a bridge as a homeless one. Are you trying to deny that Indians have been deprived of their lands?"

She brushes at her skirt with dainty fingers. "Well, no, not really. Yes, there have been grave injustices done. But our government is trying to make up for that."

"Whose government?" I ask, trying not to smile. "Mine or yours?" Yes, Blue Belle is here with me in Canada but I know where she actually resides. In the deep south. Blue Belle's country is the fundamentalist churches and town halls and call in radio shows.

Blue Belle sniffs and thrusts out her little chin. "You always try to trip me up. But you can't. Because I stand on solid rock. I stand on St. Peter's rock. I can't be moved and you know it. You want to do away with me but I am the very best part of you. Do you remember when you wanted to dedicate your life to the church?"

I search my memory. Nothing concrete surfaces. Just some vague, rather childish romantic notions of wanting to serve, but I'm not sure it was religion that stirred those longings, in fact, I am sure it was not, because I felt this spiritual yearning for connection when I was in the woods, under the trees, alone with the other creeping, crawling, wonderful growing things that filled me with awe, or in the company of other humans while exploring the swiftly flowing rivers or the sluggish, meandering waters in the swamps, full of exciting and dangerous creatures, it was life, always life, life, not death, not the death of a man who said he was God...But who knows? I could get carried away by church services when I was very young. The singing. Lord have mercy on us poor sinners.

The singing was a happening unto itself, full bodied, great hearted, chargedwith pathos and joy, winging its way to heaven. Maybe I gave my life to Jesus while not realizing it during the singing. I was, after a fashion, a believer in my past. A baptized believer. For whatever that was worth.

I'm not sure it was the church exactly," I answer finally. "It was more... oh, a search for a noble life."

Only there weren't any noble lives for someone like me who had few resources but youth and prettiness so my father in his fear for my virginity urged me on to an early marriage.

"Okay," I offer. "Well, marriage is a noble institution, right?"

"I know where you're going with that," Blue Belle snaps. "And I won't have it. For some people a life time of marriage to each other is a noble thing. You can't make fun of what your mother and father had together..."

She is working on my nerves.

"Not fun, maybe, but it certainly wasn't an ennobling experience for my mother," I answer sharply, feeling old angers buried deep within my psyche bubbling up over the way my mother, whom I loved, gave in to my father, whom I did not love. "You know why? Because she was a bigamist. She committed bigamy because she also had to stay married to Jesus Christ in order to stand my father. And she confused me in the process. She pounded into my head that a husband was necessary for a women to live an Honourable Life, especially if she wanted children and status in the community. So of course I thought nothing was wrong with marriage itself, that my marital unhappiness was the result of my picking miserable men. Of course the men I picked did lean toward the deplorable. But the underlying misery of marriage is that women must labour and love in captivity."

Well, I've done it now. Blue Belle jerks to her feet, blue eyes hot with outrage. "I can't believe you said that. I can't believe it. After all I've taught you; after all I've tried to teach you..."

I stare at her. Is she really my mother in disguise? No, Mama was a strongly built woman, not a slender little thing like Blue Belle. Blue Belle was built like...well, like me when I was young. Before old age brought all of the visual changes that it usually brings, not pretty, but somehow I like them, they keep me rooted to the ground, the way they kept Mama rooted: "my roots go down, down into the earth, my roots go down," we sang on the blockade lines.

"Blue Belle, I'm sorry, but that's the way I honestly feel," I say evenly. "Do you want me to be dishonest with you? To lie? To pretend that everything is hunky dory when it isn't? We've got real problems on our hands, health problems that affect everybody but especially children; human sperm count is dropping 2 per cent a year by some counts..."

"I've heard all that before. From you. You keep saying it. Along with mother's milk being poisoned. Do you think this makes nursing mothers feel good? You know that mother's milk is better for the babies..."

"Poisoned or no?" I ask, peering at her. She is standing at the foot of my bed, poised for flight.

"It can't be that poisoned. Children are still being nourished from it, they are still growing. These are just excuses for you to blame everything on men..."

"Yes, and on women for allowing it."

"What could women possibly do about it?"

"That's exactly my point. Women have to get power. Moral and political power. And the only way to do that is to stop pacifying men and start showing some leadership ourselves even if women have to leave husbands and boyfriends and fathers and yes, even sons..."

"Bitch has filled you with malice. I don't want to talk to you anymore."

"I'm sorry, Blue Belle. I really am."

"No. You're going to be horribly punished..."

"I already am horribly punished, Blue Belle. I am a woman and I live in a society where all of the gods are male...war gods, government gods. Education gods, history gods, money gods and of course, the Supreme God of All, Our Heavenly Father on High... Blue Belle is seething. "I think I hate you," she flings at me. And then quits my bedroom in high indignation, her voluminous skirt flouncing.

Okay. Perhaps I shouldn't have been so harsh. At least just before trying to sleep. But the scene must not have been too disturbing because I slept deeply. I woke up at a quarter to six. Coffee time. Neither Bitch nor Blue Belle were anywhere about. Relieved, I set about the day's routine with a light heart. Time to exercise, time to dance.

CHAPTER EIGHT
The Stockholm Syndrome Lives!

CHRISTMAS IS REARING ITS WORRISOME HEAD. RHODES left for Port Alberni yesterday. He has a whole other family there, consisting of his mother's husband's parents and family who he prefers to spend Christmas with. They are a lovely extended family who kept Rhodes on their family docket even after Barbara Ellen's death although their son is not Rhodes' biological father. The family lives in a rural area and go all out for Christmas. Rhodes loves the way they celebrate: the many family dinners at all the aunts and uncles, the community celebrations, the church celebrations, not to even mention the presents, while my own Christmas celebration is a grudging one.

I can't help it. I can't get beyond the commercialization aspect. Besides, the Christians stole the date from the pagans who had a perfectly good reason to make merry: the coming days would get brighter and warmer. The sun is the thing to celebrate. A Sun god sounds like a perfectly reasonable god to give thanks for and to. Well, scratch the god part, let's just give thanks for the sun. Rhodes is not into this. He's going, he says, to spend Christmas with people who really like Christmas and know how to celebrate Christmas. I waved him a cheery good-by yesterday and today I have the house to myself.

I was up at six a.m., eager to perform my exercises without fear of waking the rest of my human world. When I'm alone in the house I tear up the floor. I sing, dance, clap my hands loudly, hoot and holler and work up a sweat. It's not nice, I guess, for anybody forced to listen even through closed doors. But when I put my feet on the floor in eager anticipation of an unrestrained work out this morning the floor was unusually cold. I checked downstairs. Something wrong with the furnace.

My exercise work out this time was more to keep off the cold than anything while waiting for the magical furnace guy to arrive. In the meantime I set up a little makeshift office in front of the fireplace in the living room. At least the gas fireplace works. But the furnace isn't the only major mechanism in this house that decided to implode just in time for the holiday season. Our wonderful high tech stove that we inherited with the house had a kind of electrical spasm a few weeks ago. More like a heart attack. We are waiting for new transplant parts. From Germany. But not in time for turkey we are told. However, the family gods are working in the background. I think. Jim, my son-in-law, has offered to bake the turkey himself in his own oven. He has never dealt with a turkey before except to eat it, so we'll see. But the most fickle of my electrical friends is my computer. Four days ago it decided to take advantage of the season of good cheer and spill its guts.

So I'm in front of the fireplace trying to adjust to my makeshift office. The gas fireplace seems to be staying steady. And I do have my little netbook to work with. It's a dear, but really too tiny to be practical. I got carried away with the concept or having a computer so compact I could just slip it into my back jeans pocket when I leave the house. The problem is...well, it's like a baby. It has to have all of its accoutrements carried around with it. First, the feeding tube that is absolutely necessary. It can only go so long without electrical food. So if one is on a long bus ride or any kind of an afternoon journey one must find an electrical filling station somewhere. And the little dear must have its own pacifier and the gadget must be plugged into its side just so. This just so aspect is very important. If it isn't done to the little dear's exact demands it will have a tantrum. And of course the pacifier must be connected to a feeding source of its own that allows the baby computer to play with its toy mouse which finally gets information onto the screen, a screen that in reality, is not much bigger than a real baby's big toe, nevertheless, forget about sliding a neat little computer something into my back pocket, by the time all the wires and gadgets are dumped into a tote bag it could very well be a large diaper bag. This entire purchase was a mistake. But it's all I have to work with at the moment.

I am struck by how inappropriate it is for such a tiny machine to handle an investigation as weighty as the one I am enmeshed in. Like...are we in a phase of human evolution in which the world simply has too many men in relation to women?

Yeah. I'm beginning to think so. Certainly in some parts of China and India and Pakistan. And even here, on this continent. Traditional jobs that have been overwhelmingly filled by men are gradually falling prey to automation or to union busting corporations that don't pay men enough to even marry and start a family. Yes, it has taken two adults working to keep a home and family going especially with children for some time now, but it is increasingly getting harder. And Prime Minister Harper has prorogued parliament again.

What a sissy. That's what I think when I see his face. He tries to be so manly appearing but he is one of the biggest sissies I've ever encountered. No moral strength. No accountability. Never makes a mistake. Is always right. Whines when anybody attacks him. Thinks everybody is stupid but him. Afraid. So afraid: has to hide from the people. He knows he didn't deserve to be elected. He knows he isn't a leader. He knows, way down, that he's a cry baby.

Time to look at the second sentence of Harriet's paper on the Stockholm Syndrome. Let's see...In a state of agitation for years you start to identify with your captors...

Yes, of course. Who among us doesn't identify with their captors? The captors who generate and promote TV, all electronic toys, sports, politicians, violence...wait a minute. Those are men's captors. Women's? Okay, glossy magazines, TV sitcoms and chick flicks (how I hate that description) clothes, new appliances, new hairdos, cosmetics, children...everything about children, news programs, good works like volunteering, gossipy girlfriends, dread of old age, wanting, waiting...waiting for what? Justice? Freedom? Freedom from the approval and dictates of men? ...Freedom from captivity...

Let me read this again. In a state of agitation for years you start to identify with your captors...

Well, yes. We have to identify with our society, with our culture, or we couldn't live in it. That's why it's so hard to even see the culture. We identify with it ourselves...the sexism growing more blatant every day in all aspects of our lives, our daughters' lives, our granddaughters' lives...there is no escaping it. Okay, this is all very well, but we live in this culture, not some fairy land, and I have other things to think about.

I still have the house to myself as Rhodes hasn't returned and while my office is across the hall I find myself preferring the living room in front of the gas fireplace. God knows what my gas bill will be this month. And doggone it we can't all be like Mary Daly.

Mary Daly died on Jan. 3, 2010. Four days ago. She was born in 1928, the same year I was born. When I first heard about her twenty years ago I wasn't at all interested in reading her books. I was first searching for a kind of feminism then that was eluding me and she didn't seem to be a promising guide because she was Catholic and taught in a Catholic College.

Really, how radical can a female Catholic theologian be? But from what I have been reading about her since her death I've decided that she actually was, yes, radical. Not that I've read her books yet, but I will, and some intriguing excerpts and quotes from her have come to my attention such as:

> I came to see that all of the so called major religions from Buddhism and Hinduism to Islam, Judaism, and Christianity, as well as such secular derivatives as Freudianism, Jungians, Marxism, and Maoism-are more sects, infrastructures of the edifice of patriarchy...That revelation continues to work subliminally, inspiring my humour and stoking the Fires of my Fury not merely against the catholic church and all other religions and institutions that are the tentacles of patriarchy but against everything that dulls and diminishes women. Through me it shouts messages meant for all women within earshot: 'Tell on them! Laugh out loud at their pompous penile processions! Reverse their reversals! Decode their "mysteries"! Break their taboos! Spin tapestries of your own creation! Sin big!'

Well. What to think? Mary, I am so sorry I didn't know your works a long time ago. I'll try to make up for it in the little time I have left. I'm as old as you are, wherever you are, by earth time anyway, but perhaps not by ancient time, you are far wiser than I, you prepared yourself to use the master's tools to at least crack up his basement a bit. I am so jealous. Of your courage, your dedication. You make me seem like...oh, like Blue Belle. And speaking of the devil, Blue Belle has plumped herself down on the sofa in front of the fireplace in the living room across from me.

I'm sitting at one end of the coffee table in one of the black canvas folding lawn chairs. I love these lawn chairs. They are cheap and common, but in my opinion have a classy air with their deep bottomed canvas seats and their thin, spiderlike round metal frames. Easily folded and placed in a corner when not in use. Good engineering. With a colorful shawl placed just so around the back and sides they take on a debonair air. But Blue Belle is staring into the flames of the gas fireplace.

"I was just reading about Mary Daly's death," I say, lowering the print-out I am holding. She glances at me but doesn't say anything.

"I don't know if you know Mary Daly..." I continue. "If you knew about Mary Daly...."

"I know about her. She said she was Catholic but she wasn't really. She wasn't even Christian in my opinion. I don't know why she wasn't excommunicated."

"I don't know, either," I answer. "Maybe she was."

"No, she wasn't. At least from being a professor. She was just eased out of her teaching position at Boston College for not allowing men to sit in her classes."

It's my turn to stare. At her. Not at the fireplace.

"How do you know that?" I ask after a moment. She tosses her curly blonde head. The gas light shoots golden glints through her hair. She smiles. A smug little smile.

"I know things. You think I'm stupid, but I'm not. Witch isn't the only one who pays attention."

"I've never thought you were stupid, Blue Belle. Just wrong about ...religion."

She meets my eyes squarely. "But that would be about everything though, wouldn't it? About men, how to think about them and act toward them, about children, about how they should be raised, about sex..."

She suddenly breaks off and looks away, evidently aware that she is getting into forbidden territory.

"What about sex, Blue Belle?" I ask softly.

No answer.

"You weren't exactly crazy about it, were you?" I press. "Only a bit, at first...with you know who. When you thought you were in love..."

"I was in love that time," she says firmly.

"Or were you in love because you were...cold. Because you were freezing to death in a barren, northern town..."

"No, that wasn't it at all..."

"And you confused the hell out of everybody..." I continue, refusing to be interrupted.

"Betty, why don't you speak for yourself once in a while?" she asks, rising from the couch.

"Good point. But tell me this, Blue Belle, before you go. Which one of your four husbands will you recognize as your husband when you get to heaven?"

"None of them. Because they won't be there."

"That's funny," I say, and laugh. But she's gone. And she didn't even remind me that the Bible says there will be no marrying in heaven. Well, that's enough to almost make me want to go there, I think. If it wasn't for all that other stuff. But before I can collect my thoughts Bitch makes an impromptu appearance. She's hanging over the stair banister, smoking a cigarette.

"Put that out," I command. "You know you're not supposed to smoke in here. Or anywhere. Isn't it enough that you look like hell without stinking of tobacco, too?"

She deliberately blows a smoke ring and then saunters down the bottom steps into the living room.

"May I sit down?" she asks with exaggerated politeness. But at least the cigarette has disappeared.

"Sit if you must. But how do you know when Blue Belle is either here or has been here?" I ask, averting my face. Truly, the woman's taste in clothes is enough to make an old southern woman gag. She's got on a ridiculously short, tight, shiny lime green skirt over horizontally striped black and white Raggedy Ann knee-high stockings that reach just below her knobby knees.

"Because I'm a spy," she answers matter-of-factly. "You know that. Or maybe you don't. Your brain does seem to get rattled with corrosive amounts of sugar when little Miss Lady Bug visits."

"Well, at least Blue Belle does other things besides spying..."

"Ha," she says.

The lime green skirt slides up white, withered thighs as she sits. I try not to look. I keep my own thighs firmly under control and out of sight at all times like my mother taught me, in old age as well as when I was young. Dress is one area in which I have always been an arch conservative. Bitch just enjoys making me uncomfortable.

"And Blue Belle lives," I go on, wanting to get even. "More than you. What kind of living have you ever done? Spying on other people isn't living...you set yourself up as a kind of judge of other people, you think yourself superior, you think of yourself as...as..." I pause, searching for the right word.

"As an outsider," she answers. "I am an outsider. And a spy. I watch. And report. That's my job. What you do with what I report is your business. Once I report my job is done. Sometimes if you're not paying attention I have to report two or three times, like I'm going to do right now. Blue Belle has to go or you'll never do a damned worthwhile thing that couldn't be done by any other woman. Or man, for that matter. She profoundly distracts you and weakens your resolve. And sometimes that makes me feel like I'm wasting my time. Only you can kill Blue Belle. Make a decision on this, Kiddo. Soon."

"Kiddo?" I ask, startled. "Where in heaven's name did you hear that term? Kiddo? Jeez, that's something from even back before my time."

"Well, I'm no spring chicken," she answers, stretching out her disgusting legs. Actually, they may not have been so disgusting when she was young. They are shapely enough. Just old. "But I am getting very impatient with you. And look at Harriet's paper again. You're not absorbing it. I have to go. Try to concentrate. And straighten your backbone. Life is full of dirty jobs. I've seen a whack of 'em."

Yes, well. She gets up and saunters across the living room floor. She throws me one backward glance before ascending the stair case.

"And you told blue Belle a lie," she says firmly. "You were in love before. And it wasn't with any of your husbands."

I don't answer. I don't want to go there anymore than Blue Belle, and anyway Bitch doesn't know everything.

Bitch has disappeared up the stairs. My life is hell, I think. Kill Blue Belle? How can I do that? She's part of me; she lives in my history, in my present. I can't kill her. I just have to find some way to make her inoperable in my psyche so that she doesn't act as such a brake on my thinking, on the places my mind wants to go, the places where Bitch encourages me to go. Okay, where is that damned paper of Harriet's, her version of the Stockholm Syndrome?

CHAPTER NINE
Of Rabbits and Revolution

I FINALLY FOUND HARRIET'S PAPER ON THE STOCKHOLM Syndrome underneath a pile of downloaded articles about "drones." Drones scare me to death. But I have to stay focused on the Stockholm thing or I'll never get Bitch off my back. I begin reading from the single paper, trying to concentrate.

You are taken prisoner by terrorists. You are under extreme stress and duress.

Well, yes, but isn't everyone, men and women alike, under a lot of stress these days? Kids, too? I continue on to the third line:

In a state of agitation for years, you start to identify with your captors...

Well, can women help that? Identifying with men is all there is. Men are the only game in town. We live inside one big male brain, so to speak. Males control everything of importance on this earth. If we identify with children, with nature, with food, with music, with dance, with writing... well, men are in charge of how and under what circumstances we can do this. We can't really escape it. And even if we choose not to live with men as partners, nothing changes (except for most women, probably less money). Government, corporations, schools, churches, books, cars, electronics... the country itself was explored, defined, exploited, fought over and carved up by men. Women more or less did what men told them to. Back then. Or else.

So in order to escape "or else," women complied, had babies every other year, worked in the fields, were beaten if their men were so inclined after a bit of drink, tried to make things better for their children and died early deaths. Now, with halfway decent health care women are outliving men by huge numbers and men resent it. They really do. Just ask them. And there's this funny world map I have just discovered...

It will take a while to find it. If Blue Belle and Bitch would stop distracting me and instead help me organize, they could actually be helpful. I have too many things going, trying to market my books, find applicable case law for the court appearance in May, write "missiles" for my blog and Facebook ~ and one is due tomorrow; I try to get one in every Monday. Keep up, keep up...no matter that my computer is down and Rhodes has picked this time to go back to Victoria to stay with his father leaving me only this damned little notebook for a computer. Why can't I ever find anything?

But I turn on the radio while I am searching for the global population map. And then stop, listening. There has been an earthquake in Haiti. A very big quake. No real news yet on damage or loss of life. But stay tuned to this story, the CBC says. When did all news become stories? Maybe it won't be such a big story, hopefully; the poor people in Haiti don't need these kinds of stories. No country does, but Haiti needs a break more than some others. I have been reading about Haiti.

A book by Jared Diamond: Collapse. That's the title. Appropriate. Diamond tells us that degradation of the environment plays an enormous role in the collapse of nations and Haiti only has one per cent of its forests left. Degraded top soil, degraded water quality, scarcity of water, landslides, poor crop growing conditions...cities can turn into mud holes under these conditions or simply wash away in the rain, never mind a huge earthquake. Upsetting. I can get plumb discouraged if I'm not careful because the little efforts I make can seem so pitiful they're not worth the effort. Especially the news today from the US Supreme Court on top of the story coming from Haiti. The US Supreme Court in its wisdom has ruled that corporations are persons.

Of course we knew that already because of how corporations are allowed to use "personhood" to get away with their horrific environmental messes, their tax breaks, their preferred lending status, their ability to override environmental and civil rights of third world nations, their right to rob and swagger and compile obscene riches off the backs and bellies of the poor.

But this new definition goes even further than allowing corporate profits to override the health and welfare of people and the planet; the new ruling increases the privileges of corporate personhood, granting the same rights as actual flesh and blood citizens. The American people will now be directly ruled by the corporations, in that they can put as much money as they like into lying and brainwashing the American people. With the recent by-election to replace the late Edward Kennedy being won by a right wing republication who hates universal health care, the US is directly on the road to becoming a fascist state.

Loosely defined, a fascist state is one where corporations are so intertwined with the government and the military that it's impossible to separate them, where they use each other's offices, where the same people sit on financial boards, fill government offices, do the requisitions for the military: that's a fascist state. That's what I just told a friend on the phone. She agreed and asked, "Can Canada be far behind?"

But we concluded our conversation on a cheery note. More BC citizens are starting to hate the Olympics and the winter ski venues are melting. Whistler, a main venue, is in financial trouble and may have to close before the Olympics. But that's just a malicious fantasy; the corporate structure would not let that happen. However, on another cheery note, The Supreme Court of Canada has ruled that major corporate rearranging of the earth in BC or other provinces must have comprehensive provincial and federal environmental assessments. But we'll see how this ruling plays out. The US court ruling is more significant, as it could portend the beginning of a real American Revolution. Now where is that bloody map? And why am I even looking for it?

Oh, yes. Here it is, at the bottom of some miscellaneous papers on more court rulings. The map is from the Wikipedia site on human sex ratio. There are actually three world maps, one for the total human population average, one for humans below aged fifteen, and one for humans over 65. As I look at these maps I decide they're not so much scary as just weird. The countries with more women than men are coloured blue and those with more men are red. Light and dark shades of these colours indicate whether the male to female ratios are slight, pronounced, or somewhere in between.

According to the general population map, there are more women than men in most of the world, the exceptions being Central America, China, India, Saudi Arabia and Greenland. And I was surprised by the over sixty-five age group as I expected to find more women than men in most countries. But no, men gained ground in this map as Chile joined the more men group along with five Latin American countries. But the map that really surprised me was the under 15 years map. The entirety of the Americas has turned blue: North, South and Central American countries are blue with girls, as is Greenland, all of Europe, and Australia, with only one white spot in Africa. I haven't figured out what the white spots mean as there is no explanation but the map leaves only China red, and I mean really red.

Oh, rats, I could never read maps accurately anyway, but it seems that except for the pronounced reddening of the map in China; the blues are on the upswing. So are environmental and political events.

It is now slightly more than two weeks after the earthquake in Haiti and workers pulled a man out of the debris in Port au Prince alive, and evidently unhurt. He had been trapped underneath tons of debris with a big jug of water that kept him alive while he waited to be rescued.

Now, what kind of luck is that? People can live without food for two weeks, but not water. This man will be wondering about this the rest of his life...a big jug of water? To be trapped with the one elemental, absolute necessity for life? And where did the jug of water come from? It was obviously stored somewhere in the building.

I have called CBC about Haiti. On two different days, as a matter of fact. To The Current. I like this program; I like Anna Maria Tremonti. She is a no-nonsense kind of woman whose curiosity about the world seems genuine. I urged the program people I spoke with to educate their listeners on the environmental destruction that was profound in Haiti even before the earthquake that has been the result of deforestation. The Current either took my suggestion or figured it out, and got Jared Diamond on the phone several weeks later.

Diamond is a Pulitzer Prize winning environmental writer. He told The Current's audience that deforestation is grim news indeed, and plays a significant role in whether a country becomes a failed state or a relatively prosperous one like Haiti's neighbour, the Dominion Republic. The story of how and why Haiti's forest cover was so denuded is enormously interesting. It seems that in 1804, slaves in Haiti revolted and gained physical freedom from their French Colonial masters. However, during this time the French heavily logged Haiti's valuable old growth forests. The economic freedom the Haitians wished for didn't materialize for many reasons, and poverty stricken, they turned to devastating the forests themselves to make charcoal. That and the remaining forests were all they had left for export. So most of Haiti's formerly lush forests sailed away to France. Our forests are sailing away, too, largely in the same raw log state as Haiti's did. The only difference is that the forests of BC are not sailing to France, but to China, Japan, and the US.

I occasionally poke through a book about the Russian Revolution, given to me years ago by a friend, which I have hauled around for ten years at least. Unread. For one thing the book is horrendously thick. And heavy. With many, many Russian names. No citizens of any other country have as many names as Russians. The descriptions of the revolutionary struggles are violent beyond belief. Both the peasants' revenge on the landed gentry and the landed gentry's attacks on the revolting peasants are almost too barbaric to read. I have a sketchy knowledge of the Russian revolution, including the ending, but my God, what these people went through. It's slow going but I read the thing for an hour or so at night, plowing my way through. Tonight when I put the book down, ready for sleep, Bitch leans over my bed and picks it up.

"I wish you would announce yourself before you barge in," I snap. She flips through the book for a moment, ignoring me. Then she places the book on my night table and looks at me.

"That's heavy stuff," she remarks thoughtfully.

"Yes."

"Do you think you're a revolutionary?" she asks.

I am surprised by the question. Her deep set eyes are on my face, dark and serious as she waits for my answer,

"That's a stupid question," I answer after a long moment.

She nods. "Maybe. But you should find out. Before you die. You should know that before you die."

"Oh, for Christ's sakes," I sputter. "I'm eighty-one years old, how the hell can I be a revolutionary..."

"It doesn't have anything to do with age. It's spirit."

"I'm not smart enough to be a revolutionary!" I wail. "These people... these men were revolutionaries. And they killed so many people for their revolution. And then where did their revolution go?"

"I'm not talking about them. And I'm not talking about physical violence. I'm talking about you."

"But I can't," My voice is whiny. I hate that voice. It seems to come from outside me somewhere, a stranger's voice.

"Why can't you?" Bitch demands.

"Because nobody would listen to me. What do I know about revolution except what I've heard or read? Russian workers and peasants brought about their revolution. Ditto the Chinese. And I've never been a Cuban peasant trying to scratch out a living in the cane fields, those that brought about the Cuban revolution."

I pause for a moment, thinking about the sugar cane workers in Cuba.

"But come to think of it, I guess I was working in my father's cane fields, at least once in awhile, before he accidentally shot himself." I continue. "About the same time the Cuban Revolution was going on. But that's over. And I'm not an academic," I add hurriedly. "I don't have any degrees. Besides I'm handicapped."

Her eyes narrow to glittering slits. "How are you handicapped?"

I take a deep breath, trying to still a rising tide of rotten memories that flood into my head.

"How are you handicapped?" Bitch repeats the question. Her voice isn't loud. Or obnoxious. Just steely and insisting. I still don't answer.

"Because you couldn't colour inside the rabbit like the teacher wanted you to?" she asks finally.

I feel like crying. I wish she would leave me alone. I'm doing okay. I can write, speak, I have a voice. After a fashion. As much as any old woman has a voice in these times. I decide to stare her down.

"Yes," I finally admit. "Because of the rabbit."

"Then you're a bloody coward. You can't accept, even now, that the rabbit was a gift. Until you accept that, you'll never be able to accept yourself, and you will die hiding behind an excuse like the bloody coward that you are..."

I throw a pillow at her. It strikes the wall and bounces to the floor. Bitch throws me one last contemptuous glance and disappears. After a bit I calm down. Okay, so I have to think about the rabbit. I have to remember and think hard about the rabbit.

First grade. I thought I was going to like school when I got off the bus with my brother Ray Allen and he pointed me toward the little kids' play yard on the right side of the school. There were a dozen or so kids playing in the yard already. They came on an earlier bus. First and second graders. I knew two of the girls from Sunday School. Thelma Lou and Cindy Doughty. They were just starting a new game of hopscotch and asked me if I wanted to play. I happily accepted the invitation.

The two girls had already drawn the hopscotch lines in the dirt on the far side of the swings where the Flying Jenny pole used to be. Ray Allen told me earlier that the principal had the Flying Jenny pole moved to the other side of the school where the big kids played. To keep the younger kids off. Occasionally the third and fourth graders got the rings on the pole going too fast for the little ones. After a couple of sprained ankles and one broken tooth the pole was moved. But on my first day of school the kids in the younger grades didn't seem to miss the Flying Jenny. Kids were playing on the swings and teeter totters and it was all very jolly. The game of hopscotch went well and I was in high spirits when the bell rang and we all lined up and then marched into our respective classrooms.

I had seen the first grade classroom before. Ray Allen had brought me to school with him on the last day of school the previous year. It was the custom. All the older kids brought their younger brothers and sisters who would be attending the upcoming year. And I had already met the teacher. She was young and pretty and had only been teaching a couple of years. She seemed hardly older than the biggest girls in school but we all addressed her as "Ma'am." That's how all the women teachers were addressed. The principal, Mr. Haricot, taught the older kids math and science and was simply addressed as "Sir." So I knew how to behave properly. And Mama had already taught me to read a little so I wasn't anxious about being able to do school work.

And there wasn't any real school work that first day. We saluted the flag first and then Ma'am helped us stumble through the first lines of the pledge of allegiance to the flag. After that we sang a little good morning song that I knew from Sunday School. This little song would be laughed at today. Or banned by the Christian Right. The words were:

Good morning, good morning, good morning,
The sun shines above us today,
Let us play while we work,
Let us work while we play,
That's the way to be happy and gay.

After the song Ma'am put a marching song on the record player and we marched smartly around the room. We were all excellent at marching. But everything went downhill after that. Ma'am had one of the kids sitting in front pass out sheets of mimeographed paper with different animals outlined on them and some crayons. Colour the pictures, Ma'am instructed.

My picture was of a rabbit. I knew it was a rabbit. The outline covered more than half the page so I did know it was a rabbit. At least at some level I knew it was a rabbit. But in order to get the rabbit to appear I started colouring outside the rabbit line. This was the way I coloured at home. Mama had tried several times to convince me that I should colour the main object on the paper first. This seemed to me like a puzzling and chancy business. Like going at the thing backwards. How could one actually know what the main image was for sure, until it was squeezed out of the background? My method of colouring frustrated Mama. And at the moment, it was frustrating Ma'am.

"No, honey, you're colouring the wrong way," she said gently, leaning over my work. "You're supposed to colour inside the lines."

She smelled of lemon balm. Mama used it sometimes. Nice, comforting smell. I nodded and Ma'am moved on to the next kid. I looked at the colouring marks she had made inside the rabbit line that I was to follow. I tried to follow them with my own crayon but after a moment my head began to swim. How could I tell Ma'am that if I did it her way and tried to colour the inside of the rabbit first that this made the inside of the rabbit the same as the outside to me and this made my head swim?

All of us kids were seated at a long table. I glanced furtively up and down the table. The other kids were all colouring away. They could evidently see the lines of their animals straight, the pigs and roosters and ducks all were taking shape. Except my rabbit. My rabbit was going nowhere. I started crying.

Ma'am came quickly to my side.

"What's the matter, Betty Jo?' she asked, her voice full of concern as she leaned over me and my uncoloured rabbit.

"My stomach hurts," I blubbered. The other kids were staring. Ma'am took me by the hand and marched me into the school office. Mrs. Bronson promptly took charge of me. She was the school secretary who doubled both as vice principal and nurse. Mrs. Bronson was also called Ma'am. She was retirement age, hard of hearing, but kindly. There was a cot in the little room behind her office. "Honey, if you feel like you have to throw up, there's the pan by the cot. When Mr. Haricot gets back I'll see if he can take you home."

That prospect frightened me. Mama would be upset if the principal brought me home. And if Daddy was home he would certainly be disapproving, too, for all kinds of reasons. Daddy didn't think much of school anyway. It was because he had never been to one. They lived in the woods when he was growing up. During his childhood times there was no public education in the small town areas. White people had to pay for their kids to go to school and black kids didn't go at all. The family father deserted when Daddy was twelve years old and he went out to do something called "dipping turpentine." I wasn't sure exactly what it was when Daddy talked about it except that it was hard work. So he was working to try to keep the family afloat when he was still a child.

Daddy had a younger sister named Pearl. Some distant relatives in Baton Rouge offered to take her in and send her to school. Aunt Pearl was a big help around their house and a good student. After high school she was placed on a list of deserving students who should go on to something called Normal School and become a teacher. Which she promptly did, as she was given bursaries. When she was home during the summers and school holidays, Aunt Pearl taught Daddy to read and write and do math. It was her money, too, that helped the little family to survive.

And because Aunt Pearl was a good teacher, Daddy had a relatively good education for those times without ever going to school. Sure, he wanted us kids to go to school but I could tell he also thought too much school was a waste of time. When I was growing up I overhead him say the same thing to Mama. "If kids know how to read and write and do arithmetic, they can teach themselves whatever else they want to know," he said more than once. Mama would get mad when Daddy talked like that. Because Mama had been to college, too. She had also been preparing to become a teacher when she met Daddy.

Whatever, I knew from that first day I was different. Straight lines on paper made my head swim unless I approached them a certain way. At home it didn't matter; I drew and coloured my way. But I obviously wasn't going to be able to do that in school. I didn't want to go back to school after the rabbit incident on that first day. But Mama made me. I cried most of the time before school, the hot tears dripping onto my breakfast plate of biscuits and eggs. I could tell Mama was worried about my situation, but she made me go to school anyway.

I became terrified of school. It got to the point where I wouldn't eat any eggs and biscuits at breakfast. I wouldn't eat anything for breakfast as I would just throw it up. A couple of mornings I caught Mama crying, too, through my own tears. And then I had an accident that happily solved the situation. At least until Christmas.

I cut my foot on a piece of an old glass jar hidden in the tall grass at the far end of the back yard. The jagged glass almost severed my big toe from the rest of my foot. The glass cut through what was evidently a very important artery. Later I learned that I had almost bled to death before my parents could get me to a doctor's office that got me to an ambulance that carried me to a country hospital this side of Baton Rouge. I wouldn't have made it except that Mama knew about tourniquets and stuff.

I was much petted after I got home because of what might have been. As I recovered, Mama resumed teaching me. After Christmas I went back to school under much duress. Almost before my crying and refusing to eat campaign even could reach a crisis point, I came down with the mumps. And just as I was recuperating from the mumps Ray Allen brought home a wonderful case of chicken pox. I never went back to school again on a regular basis. I went occasionally to sit in and to visit with some of the other kids but I never went regularly. And because Mama had as much if not more education than most of the elementary school teachers in those days, along with the certificates to prove it, we were left alone by school officials.

Like Aunt Pearl, Mama was a good teacher. She knew that I had some kind of learning disability that prevented me from seeing figures, lines, and spaces the way she and everybody else seemed to see them. The difficulties in stringing words together in reading were overcome by my intense desire to know what the words said, even though sometimes whole sentences would float off into the air and it would take a serious effort to bring them back and pin them down. But once I began to master this feat, I wanted to read all the time.

Arithmetic was something else. On some days all the figures might just as soon appear backward on my paper as forward. But sometimes just the four or nine would turn around or the five would decide to appear upside down. Roman Numerals were a nightmare. We just skipped those. However I learned to do simple sums in my head, even multiply and divide a little bit, I could even make change. I could see the numbers in my head somehow, but not readily recognize them on paper. My proudest day came when I could work a problem of long division and reduce the reminders to their common denominator without left over numbers hanging out in the middle of nowhere on my work paper. I was eleven years old.

However, the barriers to understanding decimals and multiple fractions fell swiftly after that. Geometry was a different story. All those straight lines and spaces did not connect in any way to my incoming messages centers. After much frustration on Mama's part, and despairing weepings on mine, she and I made a mutual decision to put Geometry where we had put Algebra. Somewhere far, far into the future.

In retrospect I realize that I had a classic learning disability. Today it is called dyslexia. Yet in some ways, I think I had a great education. I feel I have a kind of knowledge about some subjects that is the result of following one's own interests. In turn, the interests nudged me in the direction of learning how to do independent research. But I realize that society as a whole considers me unqualified when I try to discuss issues about which I am knowledgeable, but shouldn't be, without a PhD behind my name. So how can I start, lead, or even be a part of any significant women's movement?

No. I've decided it's impossible. To hell with Bitch. She doesn't understand, she doesn't know what she's talking about. But that night brings fretful dreams of being in a war, in a bunker like a movie depicting a World War One scene...

Months have passed since that crazy confrontation with Bitch. The occurrences of major events seem to be speeding up, threatening to interrupt any peace of mind I may cultivate...

CHAPTER TEN
FrankenFish and GMO People

IT IS MARCH 17TH, 2011. SIX DAYS AGO THERE WAS AN EARTH-
quake in Japan. And a tsunami. And terrible ongoing troubles with Japanese
nuclear plants stemming from the earthquake. There are also reports that
one of their volcanoes is erupting. Japan is bearing the brunt of Mother
Nature's wrath. At the moment. Next time, us, or California, or Mexico.
But as the weather seems calm enough here in Canada so far, except that
we have had warmer winters in all provinces, how are we faring politically?

Well, some of Harper's most trusted cabinet ministers have indicated
they won't run again. Stockwell Day, Evangelical Fundamentalist Christian
from British Columbia, perhaps unnerved by the terrible events and accompanying chaos in Japan, may very well be coming home to get ready for the
"Rapture" that will come with the "End Times." Chuck Strahl, Minister
of Indian Affairs, has announced that he has asbestosis. He thinks he may
have developed this from working with logging machinery earlier in his life.
And there is no treatment for this.

But the worst has happened. Stephen Harper has been re-elected with
a majority. Four new judges will be appointed to the Supreme Court
of Canada during the next four years of Harper's rule. Harper gets to
appoint them. They will reflect Harper's religious values or they won't get
appointed. Women's right to abortion is under threat as are gay rights and
human rights in general with this turn of events. I long to talk to John
about this (my third husband and father of three of my children) as I have
so many times in the past. He is widely read and socialist, like me. In spite
of the fact that we had been divorced many years I still liked to discuss

current events and politics with him. Over the phone. We couldn't stand much person-to-person contact after the divorce. When we tried to have casual conversation in the same room it usually ended badly. Only I no longer have the option.

John died last year just before Christmas. There is no one now with whom I can exchange opinions on the discoveries and mysteries and events of the last 60 years with any real understanding. No one else still alive who was my contemporary and who knew me in my twenties. No one now who understands what it was like to grow up poor white in the south as we did, to be confronted with the extreme religiosity and racism that was prevalent in those times. And still is, for that matter. But life goes on.

My daughter Margaret and her husband sold their house in Ucluelet and bought one three blocks away from the house where Marian and I live in Merryland. And Rose Mary and her family just bought a house in another town about an hour away. Of my four daughters, three of them are now within easy reach, only Sue remains in Vancouver with her husband. Rhodes is working in an office supply store in a nearby town. Marian is still working on her PhD. My final appeal to the Supreme Court of Canada has been dismissed.

About what I was expecting. But that was weeks ago. I am still mulling over the verdict. I cannot say that I think we have a good judiciary in BC. On a scale of one to ten I would say one and a half. I have been told on good authority that most of the Supreme Court judges of BC and of Canada were corporate lawyers prior to their journeys to the top benches. Judges are supposed to represent the people, to bring justice to the people. I am reminded of Antony's speech when he said he came not to bury Caesar, but to praise him, and then went on to say, "The evil that men do lives after them; the good is often interred with their bones." The judges of BC, including the Right Honourable Beverley McLachlin, Chief Justice of the Supreme Court of Canada, who was formerly Chief Justice of the BC Supreme Court, have presided over and ruled in favour of the most heinous kinds of environmental destruction of forests, woodlands and waterways of Canada. I don't forgive them.

It's the end of July now, and we haven't had any summer yet. Not real summer. Just cool, wet, spongy days. Have a gig on Cortes Island next week. A couple more in September. I'm writing feverishly about fish on my blog.

FrankenFish bug me. FrankenFish are genetically modified (GMO) fish that were developed in their early stages by Canadian Universities. Some procedures were patented along the way, and now these patented fish are set to migrate south, so to speak. A corporation named AquaBounty is in the process of getting the okay from the US FDA to put the GMO fish on the market. However, via some weird and wonderful international cooperation, the FrankenFish eggs are staying in Canada. Fish farm owners everywhere are waiting impatiently for the patented fish monsters to be approved by the US as fit for human consumption. If approved, it will be the first live animal that is genetically altered, patented and sold in fish and grocery stores. I can't stand it. It drives me crazy.

Our flower garden is very lovely but I am feeling somewhat blue. The sun is behaving badly and I've lost my way with any sense of Harriet's paper on the Stockholm Syndrome. I have to start over. I'll go looking for it again. I keep losing the paper because I don't want to find it. It hurts my head. But voilà! The Stockholm syndrome paper reappears on my desk of its own volition the day of my 83rd birthday.

I now have the entire script firmly in my hands: okay, let's start from the top:

Stockholm Syndrom
You are taken prisoner by
Terrorists
You are under extreme stress
+ Duress
In a state of agitation for years
You start to identify with your
captors
Called general adaption Syndrom[m]
You do what you have to do
To survive — which turns to
the Love of your capture
intense identification with
their goals

You are taken prisoner by terrorists
You are under extreme stress and duress
In a state of agitation for years
you start to identify with your captors
called general adaption syndrome
You do what you have to do to survive -
which turns to the love of your captors
intense identification with their goals.

Oh, good God. This is terrible. Was this the historic bloody trail not just of First Nations people, but of all women alive today? Were women were taken captive by men in our historic past, perhaps at different times in different parts of the world, but all eventually made virtual slaves as our captors violently overthrew the matriarchy that existed even up to five thousand years ago? Could men, who had newly learned how to form in-groups that opposed women as out-groups, now, by sticking together, claim women's children, work, talents, freedoms and sexual freedom as their own?

This concept resonates with me. Something major happened back then, a great wrong, a wrong of such stunning proportions that we can't shake it off today, none of us, men or women. And how can there be any peace in the world until there is a massive peace and reconciliation between the sexes? A recognition of this wrong by men that has manifested itself in all of the rules, laws, regulations, policies men have devised and that women have had to fight all through the centuries in order to survive enough to raise children, to even breathe?

Through Harriet, am I getting close to the horrendous puzzle that has tormented me all my life as manifested in these two questions...why are so many people so poor and a so few so rich, and why do men get to bully women?

Am I getting close to answers? Are the two questions actually the same question? Blue Belle wants in on the conversation. She is tapping politely on my door.

I am working upstairs in the TV room. We don't have TV but Marian bought a 48 inch screen to watch movies. And then my regular computer screen seemed much too small. Rhodes accompanied me to the store where he worked. We bought a connector thing that hooked into my little worthless netbook which in turn connected the netbook to the big screen. And then with a regular keyboard I'm good to go. This gives me a huge screen to work with. I love it. But Blue Belle doesn't like to come into this room, and rarely does. The big screen bothers her. She pauses in the doorway.

"Must you work in here?" she asks.

"It saves my eyes," I answer. "I don't have to peer at a dinky little screen."

"But you're collecting all that radiation from electricity."

"I know and I agree we're electrified way more than we should be. But there's electric current all over the house Blue Belle, and we're probably all collecting enormous amounts of radiation from Japan's nuclear explosions. Is there anything particular you want to discuss?"

She hesitates for a moment as she brushes back a soft bit of stray curl from her smooth forehead. And then she steps gracefully into the room and sits down in the big wing chair that used to belong to John.

"Yes, there is something I want to discuss," she says after the usual flapping and patting of her skirt. I brace myself, waiting for an acceler-ated tirade against Bitch as Blue Belle knows all about the version of the Stockholm syndrome that Bitch gave me. But she hesitates again, looking past my shoulder, off into space.

"I am going to surprise you," she says in a soft, but firm little voice. "I do actually agree that women have been captured."

I look at her. I can feel my eyebrows climbing to my hair line.

"You do?"

She gives her skirt a final pat.

"I know that surprises you. Certainly women had more say back in the early days of Christianity and when one looks at Muslim women today one can only conclude that they are prisoners. I mean, to have to drag around in those hot, ugly, black coverings, one can hardly call them clothes, they are more like funeral shrouds...women like pretty things..." She pauses, waiting for my reaction.

I should have known better than to hope, even momentarily, that some inkling of what religions, all religions, have done to women might begin to seep through Blue Belle's dainty little consciousness, but no. I shrug off a little surge of disappointment.

"So only the Muslim women who wear the burka are held captive?" I ask trying to keep the fatigue of lost arguments out of my voice.

"Well, we've discussed this before," Blue Belle answers. "You don't see Christian women going round in death shrouds."

I sigh. "Perhaps not. I admit the Catholic nun's habit is not as common as it used to be, but nuns still wear death shrouds as you call them, in Catholic schools in some places in Canada and the US, and they are still the norm throughout Mexico, and Latin America, and yes, even in Europe and Africa..."

"Betty, that's not fair," Blue Belle interrupts in a quick, shrill little voice. "Those women are Catholic. And they are in a special category in the Catholic Church."

"But are they not Christian?" I counter. "Could it be the Christian women in this certain category you speak of, who wear the death shroud, as you call the nun's habit, which is so similar to what many Muslim women wear, the wraps hiding their hair, covering the female body, don't you think the nun's habit suggests the captivity of all women in the Catholic church, that a few women in this special category wear these habits so that all Catholic women don't have to?"

She jumps to her feet.

"No!" she screams. Her pretty face is twisted and angry. "Anyway, I don't care. They are not like us, they are Catholic. They are not regular American Christians. They worship idols!"

"Ah," I say, quite taken aback. "I see."

"You twist my words," she flings at me, heading for the door. "You twist everything I say."

Suddenly I am very angry myself. "Maybe I just try to put a bit of realism into your petty little twisted vision of the world!" I shout after her as she flounces off.

I am in the middle of talking to a US printing house about printing and publicizing my latest book This Dangerous Place. I have given up on the usual road to getting a script published. Which was to submit your work of genius to a recognized publishing house that says they will not read it if you are submitting to other publishers, even if they agree to read without an agent. And then wait a year or two for a reply which is usually a rejection explaining they are accepting only well-known authors. By well-known they mean best-selling authors.

Many small publishers have gone out of business, which means the large publishing houses can pick and choose from many well-known writers. These editors and publishers are so spoiled now they would look askance at a long lost recently unearthed manuscript written on ancient papaya from John the Baptist. And if God himself wrote in his usual medium (his favourite was stone) and hand delivered it to the people at the big publishing houses they would call their gophers to call the police.

There isn't any money in writing books even if one is published by a relatively well known publishing house. Unless, of course, one has authored the equivalent of Harry Potter adventures. Writing is such a labour of love. Sometimes of hate. Whatever, if it's for money, you're in the wrong business. And here is Miss Blue Belle, tormenting me to death.

I can't get my mind back on my work. And it isn't just Blue Belle. I am troubled. Jack Layton, the leader of the New Democratic Party of Canada died yesterday morning. From cancer. It is disquieting. I leave the computer and wander downstairs. Nobody is about. Marian is working in her own office upstairs and Rhodes is in the little studio out back working on his music. He does electronic music. He is a DJ sometimes when he isn't working in the electronic store. Only he says he's isn't a DJ. DJ's play other people's songs. He plays his own. I sit down in one of the chairs that came with our patio table. It is four o'clock in the afternoon. Nice and cool. A sweet little breeze is blowing. The summer is waning and I have become horribly obsessed with FrankenFish. I just posted my latest missile on the subject the day before as below:

Genetically Modified People?

Impossible? Improbable? Last year I would have said so. Now I'm not sure. Consider: we already have genetically modified salmon ready to make their debut in BC fish farms. Actually, the fish (dubbed FrankenFish by US media) are already here. FrankenFish were born in Canada at Memorial and Queens Universities in 1996 and according to Biologist Bob Devlin, many are living in West Vancouver under big, white tents across from Marine Drive. Bob Devlin studies and cares for the FrankenFish. In an article featuring Mr. Devlin in the North Shore News (March, 2011.) Mr. Devlin neglected to mention that the FrankenFish is patented.

Exactly what is a FrankenFish? In this case an Atlantic salmon that has been grown from eggs that were injected with additional genes from an eel and Growth Factor IGF-1. They can grow to ten times the size of an ordinary salmon, still containing unknown quantities of IGF-1, a hormone that has been linked to early sexual maturation of human children. A company called AquaBounty (US based) has a patent on this genetically modified salmon which is the very first animal to be genetically altered and then patented like corn and canola. The Harper government won't even tell us what GMO foods are in our groceries and even if we knew, a patented salmon is a very big jump from a patented ear of corn. But a patented genetically modified pig is not such a terribly big jump from a patented salmon as both are animals. The FrankenPig already has his papers (Revivcor) and is waiting his turn to be officially tested for market.'

As horrible as this seems worse may be yet to come. In my opinion, given the power of the super rich and the super right wing, it is not inconceivable that the genetic modification of humans is also in the not too distant future. Not for food, of course. And not even, like robots, to perform repetitive or onerous tasks that most humans shrink from performing. What is it that our medical establishment is constantly calling for that is in very short supply? You guessed it, human body parts.

Human body parts are in constant demand, especially by people who can pay big bucks for them, legally or illegally. Human eggs can be genetically modified in the Petri dish as easily as salmon eggs and grown normally in the wombs of poor women in return for food for the women's hungry families. How could genetically modified humans be engineered to benefit corporations?

FrankenPeople could be sterilized in the Petri dish, like FrankenFish, kept clean and healthy, and have extremely small brains. When called upon, FrankenPeople would perhaps have several operations to remove various body parts before they would die from the operations, or be killed, humanely of course, having served their purpose. FrankenPeople would never know they were created only to serve as body parts primarily for the corporate elite. And the rest of us?

Would we be persuaded that FrankenPeople might be okay in case we needed an organ transplant for a loved one and had the money? A lot of money, of course, because the patent holder of FrankenPeople wouldn't sell their items cheap. After all, they would argue, even though the processes of modifying FrankenPeople might have been engineered in public Canadian universities as was the FrankenFish, the holders could claim they invested enormous amounts of money in bringing FrankenPeople body parts to market. Science fiction? I'm not so sure.

We have allowed patented genetically modified corn and grains without revolt. Patented genetically modified salmon are already on our shores. The patented pig is next. At what point do we as citizens refuse to cooperate with a sick and deranged economic system that doesn't even realize how sick and deranged it is? Where is that point? Sweet mother of us all, where is that point?

Blue Belle will have an absolute fit if she finds this post, I remind myself, and she usually does. I start thinking once again about how to get rid of her. How would I even do this? I could take her out to the forest and leave her but she would just follow me back home. I could push her off a bridge. But how would that work? Blue Belle lives inside my head. Still, I must find a way to kill her off, without killing myself in the process. I will never be able to think and write clearly about women with Blue Belle trying to sabotage the process at every turn.

But several days later I am undecided again. I am distracted by news. Libya is in chaos. The HST tax in BC has been defeated by a referendum. And I am somewhat scattered by next month's schedule. I have an interview with a film producer who is making a film about the interconnectedness of the world called O World. That's okay. I can schedule that to happen when I first arrive in Vancouver. The producer said he would pick me up at the station and take me to Monika's house for the filming. And the 13th is okay. I will be giving a long talk at Douglas College in the afternoon. But it is the evening event that is worrying me.

I'm to give a book reading at Chapters but I'm not sure the books will arrive at my house in time for me to leave on the 11th, or in lieu of that, if Chapters will manage to get the books to the store at time of reading. I am very annoyed at this lack of assurance from the printing press that the books will be here. Or there. And I'm anxious about the women's party meeting on the 14th. Who knows how many women will show up. Maybe a half dozen, a dozen, three dozen...I only hope enough come to make a meeting viable.

"You're anxious because you know women don't like what you said about religions when you sent out your notice of the meeting," Blue Belle pipes up. I turn from the kitchen sink where I'm cleaning the lunch things and face her. She's sitting on one of the kitchen island stools. She's holding a copy of the notice I sent out on email about the Women's Party second meeting. I come closer to reread what I had written:

To Females of all Ages, Sizes, Races and Sexual Orientation Everywhere! Women's Party Meeting Notice! Sept. 14th at 7pm in Vancouver! Please email betty.krawczyk@gmail.com for address of meeting place and to advise of your plan to attend.

Men, it isn't that we don't love you, but we want a women's only space to organize and solidify our thoughts around what we envision for a women's party. We believe the old male dominated thinking of organizing around hierarchies and "winner take all" is killing our planet. And us along with it, including our children. We believe that women are capable of halting this mad race to the cliff, but in order to do this, we must first come together and agree on how to push many of the male imposed structures of society off the cliff first.

We must confront a banking system that is privately held, corrupt, and leading us all to the poor house. We need to confront Prime Minister Harper who believes that military acquisitions are a priority instead of the health and education of children, (or for that matter, even the repair of bridges and tunnels in Quebec.) We must devise means to confront a Prime Minister who believes that corporate enrichment is the god to be worshiped (while he is personally waiting for the Rapture) and the environment be dammed (oil sands and Asbestos.) We must also confront religious structures, Christianity, Judaism and Islam, as well as all patriarchal religions that deem women to be inferior because their gods say so. And they all do. More prisons? Prisons only work for corporations who build them and run them. We believe that if we take care of our people there will be no, or few, prisons.

As a Women's Party we will want to look closely at how our court systems work. We want to study and refute how the Supreme Court of Canada supports environmental degradation by upholding the bogus claims of logging and mining industries over the rights of citizens, including First Nations, to lead healthy lives. And we most certainly will be looking at and considering action against the right of private corporations to hold patents on the essence of life itself; the private patents on plants, fish, and other animals, described as Genetically Modified Organisms (GMO's.) We believe that as long as women are absent in the most important decision making bodies in the world we will have war, disease, both physical and mental, along with premature death accompanied by environmental destruction.

Come as a woman who understands the perils we are all facing and the need to confront old ways, old means, old beliefs, and to help devise new ways and means of living lives of equality, of health, nourishment, and peace for all. Mark your calendars. See you there. "Action is the mother of hope." Betty Krawczyk

Maybe this was a little strong, I think, pushing the paper back into Blue Belle's hand.

"You know, deep down, you shouldn't condemn Christianity," Blue Belle goes on with a smug little smile. "Christianity was the religion of your mother, your sister, your father, all of your relations..."

"Yes, and I don't see any of them anymore, do I?" I snap, turning back to the sink. "I vowed that after Mama died I would never set foot in Louisiana again. And I haven't."

"You don't have to actually be there. Your kin folks are with you every day, right here in..."

She pauses. A little too long.

"Canada," I remind her. "You're in Canada, Blue Belle."

"Yes. But our kin folk are in your blood and bones. You will never get rid of them."

The thought agitates me. I am fishing around in the soapy water in the sink for any odd silverware that might be lurking when I feel the edge of the knife. My fingers tighten around the handle. I bring the knife out of the water. My best butcher knife. If only I could get rid of her this way.

"Oh, put it down," the raspy voice of the other crazy woman living in my inner house advises from the end of the kitchen counter. I turn, still holding the knife, and stare at Bitch. She is smoking again.

"You put out that cigarette!" I command. "I am tired of telling you about the smoking. And where did you get that skirt? From the garbage can?"

Bitch shrugs, snubs out the cigarette in one of the little blue saucers on the counter, the one that holds my allotment of nuts for the day.

"Okay. Don't twist your knickers, Mama. And for your information this skirt came from your closet."

I lean forward for a closer inspection. Damn, the skirt does look familiar. It's a wildly coloured tie-dyed affair with black fringes. I haven't seen it in ages. And turning my attention back to the blue saucer I see the half-smoked cigarette is smudged into my little portion of Brazil nuts. Rose Mary told Marian that both of us should eat a scant three or four Brazil nuts a day. Brazil nuts are expensive and Bitch has ruined them. I am revolted at the sight but Bitch takes no notice.

"And be careful with that knife," she continues nonchalantly. "You might hurt yourself."

"I don't need you telling me what to do," I answer heatedly. But I'm careful when I rinse the knife before placing in back in its holder by the side of the stove.

"Well, maybe you don't and maybe you do," Bitch answered. "For instance, you think that if there's not a good showing for the women's meeting you might as well die of embarrassment or failing that kill yourself because only a few women show."

"What?" I answer irritably.

"You heard me. You think you understand other women, but you don't really. Most women are inherently spiritual but they get this confused with religion and way too many of them will just go with whatever religion they were born into. Just as you still do."

"I do not," I snap. "Can't you read what I just wrote?"

"Oh, yes, but it's superficial. For instance...when you pray or meditate and think of some power beyond you, don't you think first of God the Father even when you say Goddess, Gaia, Mother...because God the Father was put into your brain when you were a toddler. And your brain remembers."

"And you don't even have one," Bitch continues, turning on Blue Belle. "A brain, that is. Don't you have anything else to do? Like ironing your little lace hankies?"

But Blue Belle is not a coward. She stands her ground. She slides off the kitchen stool and faces Bitch. She is half Bitch's size but Blue Belle is in fight mode. Her small fists are clenched with blue eyes blazing.

"Fuck you," she flings at Bitch.

I step back, astonished. Why, I have never heard of such a thing! Not from Blue Belle. And then I have to turn and stare at Bitch in equal wonder because Bitch is laughing, deep belly laughs that shake her scrawny body. And she can't seem to stop. She is doubled over, the black fringes from the wildly coloured skirt brushing the floor. Blue Belle's face has turned bright red. At that moment I decide to postpone killing her. No, I'll wait awhile. It's not the time.

CHAPTER ELEVEN
Occupy Vancouver

IT IS NOW JANUARY 5, 2012. BLUE BELLE STILL LIVES. BITCH continues to gain strength, and now directs almost all my reading. And I have become attached to the Occupy Vancouver movement. I went to Vancouver on Oct. 15 on the first day of the general assembly in front of the Art Gallery. I spoke before roughly four thousand people. Along with another bunch of pushy people who struggled their way to the front of the steps where the microphone was. I even canceled my book reading at the library in Victoria for this opportunity. I very much wanted to connect the degradation of the environment with the degradation of our social and economic systems. I was invited back to deliver a longer speech at the end of October by a representative of the speakers' committee but I didn't actually get back to the Occupy Vancouver site until November 9th, four days after Ashlie Gough, 23, died. She died during the night from an overdose. She died in the tent she had set up in front of the Vancouver Art Gallery.

Ashlie's death was a huge downer for everybody. I hung around the native elders' tent most of the time when I was on site. The elders knew me, and of me, and I have always felt at home with First Nations people. I was asked to speak several times to the people at large during the period from the 8th to the 18th. I was distressed by the apparent amount of drug use by the people who were spending the night in the tents. Public support for Occupy seemed to decrease daily, and I felt sure the decrease had everything to do with the drug use in the camp. There had been an overdose before Ashlie Gough died and another afterward. While these two other overdoses only resulted in official medical attention, they added to the death of public support for Occupy Vancouver. And then there was the alleged biting incident that happened on Nov. 7th when police tried to put out the Sacred Fire of the First Nations.

This incident happened just before I arrived on site so my report is hearsay, but is more or less buttressed by the media and newspapers. Of course BC newspapers and media are not always reliable. Or hardly ever reliable. At least in their interpretations of events. Whatever, the evening the alleged biting incident occurred the fire had already been lit in the steel drum. There was singing and dancing and much warming of hands and feet around the cheery fire in the drum. When the police came in and demanded that the fire be put out there was resistance. The authorities began to put out the fire themselves. That's when the kerfuffle started. Some biting of at least two policemen was alleged.

In the following days the First Nations Elders decided that in solidarity with the rest of Occupy Vancouver, they would not light a fire in the big steel drum anymore. But they did set up two small well-protected candle fires on a table inside their tent. The little lights were to represent The Sacred Fire. Which the City Firemen also took umbrage with when they passed through several days later. I was the only one in the tent at the time.

"Tell them the lanterns have to go," the Fire Chief demanded.

"You tell them," I replied. "I'm not in charge of this tent."

The Firemen came back later. So did the Elders. The Elders argued the two little lanterns were symbols of the Sacred Fire and if the firemen wanted to take the responsibility of blowing out the Sacred Fires they could do that, but the Elders wouldn't. The firemen went away. Then some young non-native people with Occupy argued that the Elders should blow out the flames in solidarity with the greater Occupy Vancouver movement.

By this time it was getting late. People were cold and hungry. Barney, one of the elders, was getting hot under the collar. So was Frank, the senior elder. It was beginning to look like a real standoff. The young non-natives were arguing that the Occupation wasn't just about the Sacred Fire and First Nations, that it represented many other nationalities and issues.

The Elders argued that the Occupation as a whole should stand up for First Nations' Rights. One young non-native man said that he didn't mind being a martyr for the group as a whole, he just didn't want to be a martyr for disobeying an order from the fire department. We all had a chance in court, he said, if our lawyers could prove that the people who were tenting in front of the Art Gallery had complied with all of the fire department and health regulations.

By this time I knew that we didn't have a chance in hell that Madame Justice Mackenzie would squash a court-ordered injunction to dismantle the tents. In the first place, BC court judges hardly ever refuse a request to hand out an injunction that suggests some crowd control is needed. That, in my opinion, is the primary practice of our BC judges: to use injunctions to put down any kind of citizen protest against the right of corporations and banks to keep people compliant and passive while they are being, well...screwed.

In the second place, we are ruled on secondary levels before any kind of citizen protest even gets to the court...by faint hearts. The mayor, the RCMP, the police; the Attorney General ~ faint hearts all. Faced with any kind of mass challenge to intolerable conditions, this buttoned-up mayor, the badged and gunned up police and RCMP forces, along with The Attorney General of BC ~ all have the power to act on their own without crying to the court, yelling for the judges to come and protect them. The judges are brave because they can sentence anyone to prison who breaks one of their orders and they don't care that handing out injunctions for crowd control demeans the entire justice system.

"Then you blow out the Sacred Fire," Frank said in exasperation to the young non-native Occupier.

The young, white Occupier pulled away.

"That's not fair," he objected. "To ask me to do it."

"Why not, it's you that wants it done..."

"You people lit the fires. One of you should do it..."

"Yes, just blow them out," a small murmur arose from other non-native Occupiers gathered around.

"No. It's symbolic of our Sacred Fire. We're sure as hell not going to do it..." Barney answered bluntly.

A serious split was occurring. Regardless of how the court turned out we all needed to stick together. Neither side now looked like it would move. I turned to Ellen, Frank's wife, sitting across from me.

"If you all approve, I will blow out the flames," I offered. "But you must approve unanimously."

They all approved. With some relief, I think. I wasn't native, so it wasn't like a First Nations person blowing out the Sacred Flame, but it was a First Nations friend, an elder in her eighties, who understood the dilemma. The non-native young people stayed while I said a prayer for the Flame and what I thought it represented. I asked for guidance from the Creator for the Occupy Movement and for the people camping. I evoked Harriet's name and then blew out both flames. Everybody seemed reasonably satisfied. The young non-native Occupiers went away to find the fire marshals to explain that the fire chief's demands had been met. In the end it didn't matter to Madame Justice Anne Mackenzie. I knew it wouldn't.

Madame Justice Anne Mackenzie's reputation had preceded her as far as I was concerned. As soon as I heard that she would be presiding over our hearing that would decide if the application for an injunction to dismantle the camp be dismissed, there would be no "Faint Hope Clause" for Occupy Vancouver. In my opinion, Madame Justice Mackenzie was extremely hard on the rights of citizens, but soft on white collar crimes. Looking at some of her rulings, I considered she even appeared to be relatively soft on criminal gangs. Perhaps, I thought, some of the criminal gangs have become so clever that Madame Justice Mackenzie may associate the Hell's Angels more with white collar crime than criminal gangs. Why am I bad mouthing Madame Justice Anne Mackenzie so?

I am reminded of what Maya Angelou, the famous American poet, said: "When somebody shows you what they are, believe them."

I believed Madame Justice Ann Mackenzie had already shown me what she was, at least in her court rulings that I was familiar with before she was brought in to judge the injunction hearing connected with Occupy Vancouver. And in my opinion, they were not pretty, or just.

Madame Justice Elizabeth Bennett was different. I think Madame Justice Bennett strived to be fair and just. I had been before her myself and didn't secretly hold her in contempt the way I did most BC Supreme Court judges I had appeared before. And it was Madame Justice Bennett who was presiding over the hearings connected with the BC Rail Scandal in which two underlings in the BC government, David Basi and Bob Virk were being charged with a number of crimes connected with the BC Rail sale. The two accused said they were just following orders from the top. And Madame Just Bennett had signaled that she would be ready to allow the defence lawyers to subpoena the people "at the top" to come before the court and give testimony.

Judging by the ensuing panic, it was apparent that the "people at the top" had much to hide. This activated all the people with "too much to hide" and those whose business it was to protect the "people with too much to hide."

In short, Associate Chief Justice Patrick Dohm advised the court that Madame Justice Bennett was desperately needed over at the Appeals Court and that she should quit the Basi-Virk courtroom immediately and hop over there. Not to worry about the hearings she had been holding on the sale of BC Rail and Basi-Virk for several years, they would find a replacement for her on this trial immediately.

I had also been before Justice Patrick Dohm before. Once. He was extremely rude and arrogant. The worst kind of judge, one who would never bring fairness and dignity to BC Courts, in my opinion, because he didn't believe in citizen participation or the evolution of law. I don't think many of the other Supreme Court justices, did either, but at least they weren't overtly contemptuous of the people who appeared before them in court. They were decent enough to at least be reasonably polite to us plebeians while they were writing up their reasons for refusing to acknowledge that we protesters should have the same rights under the Criminal Code as regular criminals. For Justice Dohm, it was simply, "I'm the boss and sit down and shut up or I'll put you in jail."

Well, I was already in jail at the time and I detested his attitude. So I sassed him back, as my mother would say. In no uncertain terms. That's one thing about already being in jail. You needn't be afraid of going there. And this encounter began my association with Cameron Ward, a lawyer who happened to be in the court room that day who heard me sassing Justice Dohm. Cameron Ward contacted me the following day. He offered to try to get me out of jail without signing anything. Pro bono. I accepted the offer. I'm not sure how Cameron accomplished this as the opposition lawyers fiercely opposed, but he did.

And now in the Basi-Virk hearings, Associate Chief Justice Patrick Dohm was going full tilt in an all hands on deck maneuver to get rid of Madame Justice Bennett. Before she could do the unthinkable: allow the defence lawyers to compel Gordon Campbell and Christy Clark and a host of other "people at the top" to testify. Why, if this happened it could bring down the entire BC government and implicate God only knows what other unsavory and perhaps illegal elements that might even suggest prison terms for some of the "people at the top." No, this couldn't be allowed. The Gordon Campbell government and associates were simply "too big to fail."

So Associate Chief Justice Patrick Dohm bumped Madame Justice Bennett up to the Trial Judge Division. It was a promotion that took her completely out of the Basi-Virk trial. There were no complaints about the way Madame Justice was handling the case; Justice Dohm had to think of something. A promotion fit the bill. And then Justice Dohm parachuted in Madame Justice Anne Mackenzie who knew what she must do. That was to pass along six million dollars to Basi and Virk in exchange for their pleading guilty, not testifying against their superiors, and going home. And shutting up. Associate Chief Justice Dohm retired shortly after this trial (or non-trial) had been cleaned up to the Campbell government's satisfaction, and guess what happened? Madame Justice MacKenzie was promoted to Associate Chief justice. Of course.

Well, Mr. Dohm had to get somebody to fill his shoes and it was payback time. However, his abrupt retirement suggests that the entire drama of play pretend justice must have been very hard on him. Continuous lying is hard on anybody. One forgets what one said previously.

So I knew about Madame Justice MacKenzie from the first, and from what I knew of her record, knew that she would in no way be sympathetic to Occupy Vancouver. I am sure the lawyers for Occupy Vancouver knew it, too. And I didn't like the way the pro bono lawyers representing Occupy Vancouver were handling the application from the city of Vancouver for an injunction to clear out the Occupy tents in the first place. I had heard Cameron Ward on the radio a few days before our hearing started.

As I previously mentioned, Cameron Ward had represented me several times before in my court battles. I knew his environmental justice beliefs and how he worked and I admired his legal arguments. So before our first hearing, in an CBC interview I heard Cameron say, in answer to the reporter's question, that if he were defending us (at the time he was busy defending many First Nations families who were demanding answers to why so many First Nations women disappeared from the Downtown Eastside in Vancouver for years without the police investigating), he would ask why the police did not just order the tents removed under threat of arrest. And he would ask why the mayor, who also had the authority to order the police to order the tents removed, didn't take that action instead of going to court and asking the Court for an injunction. This corresponded with my own thinking.

When I told the lead lawyer in the hearing the first day that I wanted to speak to the Court as a self-represented person he put me off. So I had to ask the court myself. And I stood up in court and told Madame Justice Mackenzie that there were those of us connected with Occupy Vancouver who were unrepresented, but would like to speak. The lead lawyer on our side didn't like this, and remarked that if I spoke the hearing would last three weeks instead of three days.

That wasn't nice. It fact it was outrageous and totally unprofessional. Madame Justice MacKenzie only mildly rebuked the lawyer. However, she did include me as a defendant. Which meant she might allow me to speak briefly. The paper work involved with doing this was complicated by the fact that my wallet had been stolen the evening before.

And of course every single piece of identification I had except for my passport which was back in Merryland. And the two hundred dollars that had been in my wallet was also all the cash I had. What a dilemma. No money and no identification that would allow me to get some. Nightmare time. Fortunately one of the tellers at the bank on Commercial Drive knew me well enough to vouch that I was who I said I was so at least I could get into my checking account. Not that there was much in there, either. But at least there was enough to keep me from having to ask friends for a loan or call Marian or Rose Mary to send me enough money to get home on.

It didn't really matter anyway. Madame Justice Anne Mackenzie did her duty to uphold the bias of the law in British Columbia against free speech and free association. After the injunction was granted and everyone was ordered to dismantle their tents there was a lot of disbelief at first.

I think many of the young people actually thought they had a chance to overturn the injunction if they were all good kids and complied with the fire and health regulations which they had done. Keen disappointment. And disillusionment. Much depression. The following day people were taking down tents, but there was music on the stage to try to cheer people up. And it was Aboriginal Day.

I was scheduled to speak, so I went early to the Art Gallery, where several First Nation drumming groups were already setting up. That was special. The drumming and singing, complete with a couple of fancy dancers, was wonderful. When it came time for me to speak I talked about Harriet Nahanee and the Red Legged Frogs.

Harriet told me about the Red Legged Frog not long after we were first arrested at Eagleridge Bluffs. We had been released on a promise to appear for trial. Harriet called several days after the bulldozers and other heavy machinery moved into the Bluffs to clear the Arbutus Forest for the multilane highway that would make it an estimated three minutes (or was it ten?) faster driving to Whistler for the Olympics. When Harriet called she said she was going back to the parking lot at Eagleridge Bluffs where we were arrested. When I asked why, she told me that as an elder in her tradition she had to go back to the Bluffs and sing death songs and prayers for all the dead and dying things up there. She said the migrating birds might migrate somewhere else, but the deer and bear would perish without their habitat, as would the wet land creatures.

I argued. The woman wasn't well. She had been on the blockade with us in the parking lot for weeks. She was just recovering from the flu then, and I could tell that she sometimes had trouble breathing. I told her she would be arrested again and this time they might not let her go until trial. She was adamant.

"I have to, Betty. You just don't understand. I'm an elder. I'm a Pacheedaht. I'm the only elder involved. I have to sing the songs and say the prayers. It's my duty."

"Then do it from here," I urged. "I'll meet you. We'll go to a park somewhere, or some other spot that's quiet, maybe down by the ocean..."

"No, no. It has to be there. At the Bluffs. Where it is happening. Especially when I sing for the Red Legged Frog. He is there. In the wetlands at the Bluffs."

"Harriet, the Red Legged Frog isn't the only creature that is in danger of extinction..."

"I have to go, Betty. In our beliefs it is the most important...we believe that when the last Red Legged Frog dies all of humanity will die."

There was a long silence. I couldn't think of a reply. It stood to reason. The Red Legged Frog lived in the wet lands, the marshes, the same place where it is believed that humans, or ancestors to humans, probably hung around when they first came out of the sea. Why, the minerals in our blood are still in the same proportion of minerals as in the sea...the wet lands that I remembered in Louisiana were gone...the land dried up, the water now silted and salty...I remembered. We lived not far from the bayou marshes spawned by the Mississippi River that overflowed with life: there were catfish in the shallows, crabs, shrimp and crawfish, frogs; but there were snakes, too, water moccasins and even rattlesnakes; although most were shy and would run if given a chance, still one had to be careful...

All gone now.

Even before Katrina. The area where we once lived outside Baton Rouge is now drained and filled in; there are subdivisions, and oil rigs, casinos, nothing is the same. When Katrina came there was nothing to hold her back, no bayous, no wetlands, no...frogs. Not like there were before. Not the big fat toads, the enormous croaking bullfrogs that frequently lost their hind legs (and their lives, of course) not only to Cajun supper plates but to some of the finest restaurants in Baton Rouge...

"Okay," I said to Harriet after a long moment. "But wait for me. I'm coming with you."

We went the following day. It was Sunday. Usual west coast early summer day; mixture of sun and clouds. When Harriet and I met in front of the parking lot we saw immediately that the place was crawling with cops. There must have been half of the West Vancouver Police force there to greet us. Okay, a slight exaggeration. But the powers that be weren't taking any chances of another interruption in the dismantling of a rare urban forest. The police followed us to the foot of the Bluffs and surrounded us. The workmen stopped their machines. The earth just above the parking lot had already been made into a marshy mush, boulders removed, priceless Arbutus trees downed, distressed sea birds shrieking their panic and disapproval overhead. Harriet started singing the songs for the dead and dying in the Pacheedaht language, softly at first, then louder, her voice throbbing with grief and anger.

I don't know how long Harriet sang. Time seemed to stop. I couldn't know the actual words she was singing, of course... but I knew...I felt the depth of her voice, her vision, the sorrow and rage she felt, I was being swept into something I hadn't witnessed before, but I knew...she and I were sisters, a shared sisterhood that I felt more deeply than I felt for many of the non-native women I knew, something that went back, way back, something ancient, something women shared thousands of years ago, before the male vision overtook that of the female voice, when there was the mother rule...

But then Harriet suddenly stopped singing. She prayed, briefly, hands outstretched. And then it was over. We were ushered out of the parking lot by half a dozen policemen or more.

The prayer service was hardly noticed by the press even though we were technically breaking the law. As much as I had always courted the press in order to get people to question why I was doing such outrageous things, for once I was glad not to be noticed.

After all, I seemed a rather normal, even nice old lady. But all that publicity around my blockading actions raised questions...was I a megalomaniac of some sort or did I actually believe our trees and waters and lands were being devoured so quickly and systematically that I was willing to endure prison to protest? Were things really that bad?

But I was glad I went with Harriet that Sunday, and to have our forbidden visit to Eagleridge Bluffs go unnoticed, except for the police, because while it was public, it was also a private thing for me, one that I hadn't quite digested. By the time I did digest it several months later I was already in prison and Harriet was dead.

While I spoke of Harriet in front of the Art Gallery to the Occupy gathering I felt her presence keenly, as a knowing, if she were still alive, she would also be at Occupy Vancouver, kibitzing in the Elder's tent, telling stories, laughing, giving interviews.

But Occupy Vancouver has been dismantled and scattered. And I'm back home in Merryland. It is now Jan.23. Tomorrow is Rhodes' birthday. His twenty-first. Marian is away but I have invited Margaret and Andre over for cake and ice cream tomorrow evening when Rhodes gets home from work. Marian and I have made a decision. It is a big decision. The other girls don't know what to make of our decision and I haven't even told my sons yet. And Blue Belle is having a continuous series of fits about it.

Marian and I have decided the house is too much for us. She is away at least half the time and I am rather isolated when she is away. This house is beautiful but it needs more people. Marian takes her car with her when she travels. I don't drive anymore anyway. I love the wilderness but I've always had trouble with village style towns and I'm too old to just go hiking up a mountainside by myself. Or even with companions, for that matter. Maybe these are just excuses. The people are lovely but I'm bored with the village.

Marian is also restive. She thinks I try to boss her and she has the tendency to be overprotective, to treat me like I am one of the frail elders she studies. I frequently contradict her. She finds me a pain in the ass. I have decided that as long as one is healthy and independent it's a mistake to live with one's adult children, regardless of how wonderful they are. And I would like to go somewhere I can afford for some sustained sunshine for a couple of months a year. Blue Belle thinks I am mad and informs me that she may refuse to go with me to California where I have relatives. This would save me from having to kill her.

CHAPTER TWELVE
A High Wind Brewing

I HAVE CHRONIC INTERMITTENT POSITIONAL VERTIGO. Which means that my inner ear goes wonky once in a while and makes me dizzy when I move my head suddenly. Which has just happened. Blue Belle has seated herself in the empty chair across from me. We are in the TV room. I think I have mentioned before that while we don't have TV we do have an enormous TV screen. It's hooked up to my little netbook computer. It's great: I can actually see what I'm writing on the 42 inch screen. Hoffman, Marian's cat, who has been deep in kitty dreamland while snoozing on the ottoman senses Blue Belle's presence. She lifts her head, wide awake now, and stares in Blue Belle's direction. But I wait a moment for the dizziness to settle before I gingerly turn my head to also focus on Blue Belle.

"See, what if you have a bad case of vertigo in California," she says in an accusing voice. "Who would take care of you?"

"I can still take care of myself," I answer evenly. "Right now Marian is at home and I haven't even told her I'm having a bit of vertigo. It goes away on its own. A few days are all it lasts. Besides, the only thing that actually helps it is that Chinese tea I got from the Chinese doctor in Victoria. Surely I can find some of that same kind of tea in California. You remember, don't you, the Chinese doctor who told me that the inner ear is connected to the liver and that the liver is the seat of anger and that I had to find some way to let my anger out in peaceful ways..."

Blue Belle sniffs. The drapes in the room are pulled back and wow, the afternoon sun suddenly breaks through the shifting dark clouds and splashes across Blue Belle's bright, curly head. She looks so young, I think.

Like a doll. Like a petulant doll. My heart warms as I gaze at her. Why on earth would I wish her dead? With a little luck she will refuse to go with me to new adventures in California next year for a little while and will just disappear into her room and shut the door behind her, forever. She takes a deep breath and then daintily touches her forehead with the little white handkerchief adorned with the pink embroidered edging. And then sits down in Daddy John's chair with the usual fussing with her full flouncy skirt.

"Why can't we go back to Louisiana?" she asks after a moment, looking at me. The little familiar frown creases her forehead. She seems a trifle nervous. Or more agitated than usual. Her delicate fingers are busy rolling the hankie of the day into a ball in her lap. I stare at her fingers fussing with the handkerchief ball for a long moment. I have never seen her do this before with any of her handkerchiefs which mostly serve as small dainty wisps of theatre.

"Because there isn't any Louisiana," I answer slowly. "Not the way it was before back when there was some hope, when there was Martin Luther King and the Kennedys. And right now it's really ugly, with Newt Gingrich trying to rile people up by suggesting that welfare is just for lazy black people and they should all just get jobs when there aren't any jobs..."

"But it's always been like that," Blue Belle breaks in. "Even when Martin Luther King was alive, and now there's Barack Obama. He's half black..."

"And the other half is white. Blue Belle, it's no use. We are not going back to Louisiana. I never want to see Louisiana again. We may go to California for a few months next year and that's final."

Blue Belle jumps up, the handkerchief ball rolling onto the floor. Hoffman activates. She jumps from the ottoman and pounces on the ball as it rolls under Blue Belle's chair.

"But why?" Blue Belle demands. "So you can associate with whole bunches of godless people, with atheists, with women who want to kick men off the planet? I'd sooner die than go with you!"

I stare at her. She is in a state. Before I can think how to calm her somebody else appears in the doorway. It's my daughter Marian.

"Who are you talking to, Mom?" she asks. Hoffman provides an answer. Hearing Marian's voice she scrambles out from underneath the chair where she has been chasing the handkerchief ball and hurries to her mistress.

This cat has to be right up there with the world's most spoiled cats. If she is separated from Marian for more than a few minutes and Marian reappears, the cat will run to her meowing piteously as though Marian had just saved her from some kind of imminent death.

"Oh, you were talking to the cat," Marian says, answering her own question. Then she stoops down to pet her darling.

"Do you need me?" I ask, glancing somewhat furtively at the other side of the room where Blue Belle had sat. I knew Blue Belle wouldn't be there, it was just a nervous reaction.

"I have to run some errands," Marian answers, glancing up after assuring Hoffman that her world is not going to end within the next five minutes. "Do we need anything from the grocery store?"

"Yes, a few things. I'll make a list. I just have to finish this first," I say, nodding at the computer. "I'll be down in a moment."

"Okay, Mom..."

Marian scoops up the cat. "But you come with me, you bad kitty and stop bothering Grandma..."

Get that. I'm Grandma to a cat. Rose Mary does the same thing. She'll instruct their dog Ozzie to, "Go tell Grandma to throw the ball for you..."

As soon as I hear Marian's feet hit the bottom steps downstairs I hurry over and lift the skirts of the chair Blue Belle just vacated. And then breathe a crazy little sigh of relief. The handkerchief ball isn't there. Blue Belle took it with her. I suppress a giggle. Why, the very idea, my thinking the hand-kerchief ball could possibly be real, that it might have remained under the chair. The suppressed giggle bubbles up again but I quickly swallow it back. I really, really do have to get rid of Blue Belle, I decide. Her voice inside my head might cause me to go to the elder Looney Bin before I can make it to California. I have to deal with her. Soon.

Of course Bitch is pleased with my California decision. Later that same evening after I've retired for the night, Bitch visits me in my bedroom.

"So Harriet's Stockholm Syndrome finally bored its way through your thick skull and found your brains," Bitch says. Her little half smile is as condescending as Hoffman's triumphant smirk.

I am annoyed. Bitch and Blue Belle are both increasingly trying to break through my boundaries. It's only nine thirty. I might read until eleven before getting sleepy so I have propped myself up in bed with an opened book by my side. Neither Bitch nor Blue Belle ordinarily appear when Marian is about. But Marian is busy watching a video on her computer in her own bedroom down the hall. Our different tastes in film usually prohibit our watching a movie together. Bitch is leaning against the sliding glass door that leads out to the little balcony off my bedroom. A sudden, startling whistle of wind lashes against the window.

This lousy weather has been going on for three days; icy rain, intermittent loud gusting winds, and when the wind and the rain take a breather, a soft powdery snow falls that almost immediately turns into streams of mushy little ice rivulets that cascade down the windows and glass doors.

I adjust my pillows, trying to hide my annoyance at Bitch's untimely visit. The book I'm currently into is lying open on the bed. Hoffman wanders in. She ignores Bitch, jumps up on my bed, and immediately starts sniffing around the open book. Hoffman just can't resist an open book if she can get at it, in spite of my fussing about her love of provoking me. She will plump herself across any open book I put down on the bed or floor, or coffee table, then sprawl across it and refuse to move peacefully. It's her form of peaceful civil disobedience. When I take an extra book to bed and open one just for her so I can read the other peacefully, she stalks off, insulted. I look over at Bitch slouching by the glass door that leads to the balcony.

"I think you should get away from the door," I say, reaching for my book before the cat can pounce. Too late. Hoffman has already sprawled across the open pages, gaining possession. Then she starts to purr. Having won the war, she is offering peace. But on her own terms. Her tail communicates her final offer. Swishing her black tail around forcefully, Hoffman stares unblinkingly into my eyes. She is waiting to see if I will try to forcefully remove her. I realize it is too late now, that whatever path I choose to regain my book will be registered as defeat in Hoffman's challenging round green eyes. If I try to slowly and gently remove her sprawled body from across the book she will resist by digging her claws into the surrounding covers. If I remove her quickly, with a certain force, that is, a little bounce from the bed, she will turn and stare at me for a long moment with utter contempt in her eyes. And then she will stalk off in high indignation that she has to live with such a degenerate. And immediately find Marian and communicate to her that I have been unfriendly, in fact, beastly. Yet I can't let the little monster just take possession of my books this way, how can I allow myself to be vanquished by a cat, I ask myself. Still, I decide that perhaps it's best for family peace to let the cat have the damn book.

"That wind is kind of crazy," I say, turning my attention from Hoffman and her successful coup back to my visitor. "I don't like the way it's whistling."

"It's nothing but a high wind," Bitch answers, but she moves away from the door nevertheless and sits down at my dressing table. Or what used to be a dressing table. There's a small TV screen and a DVD player on one side of the table where I started to try to make sense of some of the blockade footage I had accumulated over the years. But that task didn't last long. After looking at half a dozen video tapes and a half a dozen DVD's I found the footage all jumbled up with news clips and endless shots of the ground, the backs of people's heads and feet, unrecognizable places and events... terrible mess. It would take a professional editor to glean the wheat from the chaff. And there is a lot more chaff than wheat. Oh, some day.

Cuddled up next to the DVD player is a jumble of papers, books, a pin cushion, pens and pins, two small vinyl boxes holding a bottle of tea tree oil mixed with olive oil, some foundation, lipstick, a glass of water. Even Bitch finds it a bit much. She had the nerve once to comment on the messiness of my table. But not this evening. She has something else on her mind. She turns sideways in the chair so she can face me. She just looks at me for a moment, gets up and walks to the glass doors again, and then disappears through the doors, out into the night. Strange. And disquieting. Bitch obviously had something on her mind. But if there is one thing I'm sure of it's that she'll be back. I turn out the lamp and settle for sleep with the wind still whistling and Hoffman still in possession of my book.

CHAPTER THIRTEEN
China, Christianity and Islam

I HAVE DECIDED THAT I DESPISE HILLARY CLINTON. AT ONE time I was excited that she might become vice-president of the United States. But when I saw her today on the internet on the Democracy Now program with Amy Goodman, it was like seeing Hillary for the first time. The real Hillary Clinton. Like the first time I saw Bill Clinton during the aftermath of the Monica Lewinsky affair. The real Bill Clinton.

When Hillary Clinton became real to me on Democracy Now, she was tapping her fingers on the desk before her impatiently, imperiously, her features twisted in a sneer. She was supposed to be listening politely to the Russian representative trying to explain why Russia had vetoed a motion that would have condemned the Syrian government for the war in Syria without citing wrongdoing by the opposition fighters. I decided Hillary Clinton was no longer on my list of freedom fighters. She was always just a "maybe" anyway. She was tentatively on that "maybe" list primarily for her good works in Arkansas when her husband was governor in the 1970s. And for her book It Takes a Village. But now this image of her sneering contemptuously while the Russian delegate was speaking at the UN will remain fixed in my memory alongside the image of her husband when he publically insisted to the American people that he did not have sex with Monica Lewinsky. Like a blow job wasn't sex. And in the Oval Office? While he was on the phone, presumably taking care of the nation's business as president?

The US is blatantly hypocritical concerning what is happening in Syria... as if the US hasn't propped up every bloody dictator known to man and woman in the past hundred years and is still doing it. All they want is Iran's oil while they try to hem China in. Syria is the road to both ambitions. And while I'm mad at China for buying raw logs from BC and encouraging the horrible practice of "fracking" shale gas fields in our province, I do think the Chinese are much more sane than Americans and Canadians about some things. For instance, religion.

The Chinese get it that patriarchal religions are not good for people, especially their own people. They understand that the ancient religions that separate people into opposing camps and demand that people in one group feel compelled to make other groups recognize that theirs is the only real and true god, and that all others are worse than mere fakes, that they are actually evil, then this cannot be a good way to arrange society. Obviously, it is not good, because some who hold these religious beliefs stand ready to kill dissenters, if not in actual deed, then by condemning unbelievers and their particular religion to an everlasting hell. Some groups take their religion super seriously and if you don't accept their god they may prefer to kill you in this life, rather than wait for the next.

Yes, I do believe that since their revolution, the Chinese leadership has continuously understood that "religious faith" as offered up by patriarchal religions, is enough to make men aggressive and stupid and women fearful and stupid. Not that I think the Chinese are smarter that other people as a whole, just some people. And I understand (from China Daily) that the Chinese government just sent out rather large amounts of money to be divided among the Chinese people as bonuses. There are so many people that when divided up, the individual bonuses probably didn't amount to a heck of a lot, but it was certainly a nod to sharing the wealth. A crowd pleaser. This should count for something.

There's hardly been a let up in the rain and cold of our grey February days. This old house still needs lots of heat. Our furnace gave up the ghost and we now have a new one. Since yesterday. It was so long before the men came I had become acclimatized to the gas fireplace and a couple of oil heaters. Amazing how quickly people can get used to a changed situation, if it's gradual enough. All tyrants know this.

The frog in the frying pan is a good analogy...no, I think it is a pot of water that the frog gets plopped into and instead of hopping out of the water is led on to death as the lovely warm tub gradually heats to a boiling inferno. The frog is lulled because it's all so gradual. Anyway, this is the version of the frog story recited by most as the major analogy of getting dumbed down and deadened by gradualism. But my mind hears cooked frog and immediately frames the image of frog legs simmering in a frying pan. Anyway, it's only when people's backs are completely against the wall that they will take any action. And then it's usually wildly emotional, hastily planned.

February 5th, 2012 I just listened to a YouTube of a long lost tape of Malcolm X speaking to students at Brown University. It is a recently discovered tape, one that nobody even knew existed, uncovered by Brown student named Malcolm Bumley. As I listened to Malcolm X speak, I was reminded of a speech I had once heard given by Stokely Carmichael. Carmichael was also a prominent young black activist during the fifties and sixties civil rights movement. He visited Louisiana during the voter's registration marches that were designed to try to help southern black people register to vote.

I was struck by the similarity of the speeches. Both young black men recounted the old wounds of slavery, focused attention on how the white male establishment considered black people inferior, that black people looked different, had been slaves, were not sufficiently educated, were poor, were infantile. But had "woman" or "women" been substituted for "black" in these speeches, both men would have also been describing the position of most women the world over. Especially in the speech Stokely Carmichael gave to a black audience on the subject of religion.

That was a great speech. Carmichael told the audience that they should give up Christianity because it was a slave religion. He told them that every time a black man or woman knelt before a white god that they were denying their own black beauty, power, and grace. If in their minds they considered all that was wonderful and powerful to be white, they would never rise up and claim their own skins, that black was beautiful, that black was powerful, that black was noble and did not need a slave religion. It was a very powerful speech.

I mulled over this speech later, thinking, "Stokely Carmichael dear, you got one convert from that speech. Me." I see now that as long as women kneel before a male god we are denying our own femaleness, if we think that all that is beautiful, powerful and good resides in the male figurehead, we are on the losing end of the deal. And by the time that voter registration was over the church I attended was minus one member. Me.

That was a long time ago. Of course it wasn't just Stokely Carmichael's speech that drove me from the church but it did help pave the way for both Bitch and Blue Belle to enter my life and thoughts. Whatever good they will eventually do I have no idea.

I do know that there seems to be nothing able to stop the environmental destruction of British Columbia. The oil pipeline and shale gas extraction that is gearing up to roll over Canada will tear up this province on top of all the logging and development. Not to even mention the mass acres of forests that have just given up and died because the weather has changed so. Winters are no longer cold enough to kill off the pine beetles, so they are killing huge swaths of trees, which is not doing the logging industry any good. And Christy Clark is getting bad advice about everything...what is to be done?

Not much. Harper is over in China as we speak kissing what the US at one point called the "yellow peril" and while he may mention Syria I would bet that he is going slow on advice in the matter. Nor will he refer to the Chinese government as "Godless Communists" while he is there. Which of course they are. As a post-Marxist I don't necessarily consider this a bad thing. What is so shameful is that Harper does, but he is kissing nevertheless. My, what a little time does to political alliances.

But our Prime Minister returns triumphantly on February eleventh with a fistful of economic agreements with China. I think I understand the Chinese to a degree. They know what they want and are willing to pay for it. They don't go into other countries bombing everything in sight in order to get their oil as the Americans do. The Chinese don't want to tear up their own country environmentally if that can reasonably be avoided, but yes, they are quite willing to pay the Canadian government to tear up ours. I just sent a missile to my blog on the subject. For Valentine's Day.

HAPPY VALENTINE'S DAY CANADA

Your Prime Minister has just proved how much he loves you. Panda Bears! Next year while we watch these adorable natural wonders with awe and even love, we might be able to forget for a little while what we have paid for them. Like our national sovereignty. In exchange for Canada's resource reserves, especially the oil sands and shale gas deposits, China and private investors will reap billions of dollars in addition to the long term sales of the oil and gas. And what do we citizens get? Aside from the rise in domestic oil and gas prices? And irreparable ecological damage?

Why, the loan of Panda Bears. Sweet as they are, two Panda Bears are not worth the rapid acceleration of the ecological trashing of Canada. The place where we Canadians all live. So what, some might ask. Better to be under the economic heel of a country far away than one almost in spitting distance, one, they might add, that is getting queasy about Canada's "dirty oil." The Chinese are not so finicky.

Perhaps. But these new developments are more than a little scary considering our Prime Minister's rapid turn toward China after his utter disdain of that country during his first years in office. Unsettling, too, is Harper's apparent total disinterest in, and perhaps disbelief in, any value added treatment of these same resources he has now signed away. But this has long been the federal and BC provincial stance on logging so why am I surprised that Canada will simply be shipping out oil and gas in the raw state without refining in Canada?

I guess I thought in spite of being an end times fundamentalist religionist, that Harper could figure out a way to encompass value added principles to Canada's oil and gas reserves. But apparently not. And this is a signal, in my opinion, that Canada is soon to become (actually has been becoming for years) as Alvin Toffler describes in his book "Powershift," when speaking of the future…"The backward republics, (those who are) still dependent on agriculture and raw material extraction, may huddle together in a loose federation."

As Canada certainly looks more and more like a backward republic of this description, who would Canada huddle with? Even drug war ridden Mexico has nationalized its oil reserves. In addition and largely ignored by the press, there is a global political elephant in the room as Harper invites China to draw a ring around the gas and oil resources of Canada. This political elephant is Iran and Syria. Both China and Russia seek to protect Iran and Syria. We are fed daily news updates (propaganda?) about how the Syrian government is killing its own people. However, the opposition forces who are led by the Muslim Brotherhood, also have its own army and apparently lots of ammunition. Which begs the question…is this really an uprising solely by unarmed citizens in Syria who are yearning for freedom, or is this a civil war with the opposition spearheaded, at least at the moment, by the Muslim Brotherhood?

Whatever the truth of that conflict, the US is in full battle gear lusting for a "regime change" in both Syria and Iran. The main thing stopping the US from invading these two countries is China. And with Harper suddenly China's best friend, it is no wonder that Canada hasn't recalled our ambassador to Syria as many of the European nations have done to demonstrate their displeasure about events in Syria. Recalling our ambassador from Syria might upset China no end. In fact, I suspect an agreement on this was part of the "done deals" of the economic (as yet) agreements Harper brought home. And I would probably faint (delicate flower that I am) at some of the names that Harper is presently and privately being called by the American heads of state and military. I find it rather ironic that Stephen Harper's cozying up to China, while bad for Canada economically and environmentally, may help avoid Word War Three.

Because in spite of the deaths and confusion in Syria, I am hopeful that there will be no "regime change" invasions by the US or Israel. With China and Russia both opposed this would be madness. It could very well precipitate World War Three. And if we look at the mess left in Iraq and Libya by "regime change" which was fuelled by US propaganda and outright lies, I personally don't believe much the US government says about anything, much less about a country with a path to Iran's oil. Neither do I believe Stephen Harper's stories about what he said to the Chinese government "in private" about human rights. And to top it off, I don't much believe CBC reporting on any of these matters to be unbiased. Not anymore.

What I do believe is that if Harper's plans do go through, he has sold us so far down the river as "hewers of wood and drawers of water (and oil and gas)" that there is probably no returning. But they (the Harper government, China, private investors) can take it all from us easy, or they can take it hard. Let's make it as hard as we can. Let's make it so hard they might pause to reconsider a few things. Like the Canadian people. Like the environment.

And that's possible. Happy Valentine's Day. And Panda Bears, you darlings of nature, we do love you.

And I included an enchanting photo of two Panda Bears.

"And you're going to get into trouble saying those things," Blue Belle says, peering over my shoulder to read the writing on the computer screen. I'm not using the big screen upstairs so she has to breathe down my neck to see the words. I turn and stare at her. She is becoming as brash as Bitch.

"I wish you wouldn't just sneak up on me," I complain.

"That's about the only way to get your attention these days," She says unapologetically. "And you are going to get into trouble with that."

"In trouble with what?"

She gives a little nodding jerk of her head at the screen. The curls bounce around from the motion. Sometimes she reminds me of Shirley Temple. Like when Shirley Temple was a child star, tap dancing around with Bo Jangles.

"You know with what. Writing about Syria and Iran as if you championed them."

"I'm not championing them. But I'm saying I think what's happening in Syria is more of a civil war and I hope the US doesn't go in there because it could very well start a third world war, and the opposition in Syria is being led by the Muslim Brotherhood which is also bad news for women..."

"Just stay out of it."

"Oh, for Pete's sake. At some point women have to stand up and try to figure out the truth of things..."

"Leave it to the men. They do the fighting anyway."

"Yes, and so do women. They do the dying, too, along with their children and they get raped in the bargain..."

"Well, it's mostly those heathen men over there in those backward countries who rape..."

I hang my head.

"Blue Belle...didn't you hear the American women on the CBC radio program a couple of days ago talking about how so many female soldiers are raped and harassed by their own soldiers? Didn't you hear that, for God's sake?"

"Those radio news announcers just exaggerate things to make it all sound sensational," she answers. "It's good for ratings. Don't write anything more about all those uprisings over there, it's not really going to affect us, the Good Lord wouldn't let anything bad happen to us..."

"Blue Belle, you are not a sane woman," I say wearily and stand up rubbing my eyes. My eyes are not what they used to be, especially when I log in too much time on the computer. But when I open them again Blue Belle is nowhere to be seen. Relieved, I turn my attention elsewhere.

To a National Post article (May 9, 2010), by Juliet O'Neill of Canwest News Service, under the following headline:

"The average Canadian would not object to the use of intelligence potentially obtained by torture if it means saving Canadian lives, a senior official at the Canadian Security and Intelligence service suggested Wednesday."

The senior official was Michael Coulombe of CSIS (Canadian Security and Intelligence Service) speaking to a Canadian parliamentary committee.

Getting to know you, Canada. The new you. Getting to be so like the country I left in disgust during the Vietnam War. Yes, that country. That war loving country. Iraq, Afghanistan, Libya...these were secular states before American invasions. Now they are sinking back into the arms of fundamentalist Muslims and women no longer walk freely midst guns, bombs, fatwas, women's clothing police, sick children, lack of nourishing food and clean water. Oh, yes. God bless America. Bless their guns, tanks, bombs, drones.

Yes, I am restless. I need more information concerning what I want to explore, what I want to research. I need to learn more. I need more clues about how women are still held captive even when we seem to be enjoying a certain amount of equality in the western world, even when we refuse to recognize our captivity, how this lack of recognition runs so deep we come to love our captors, and to intensely identify with them...

Like the book I've had to wrestle away from Hoffman several times when I retire to read in bed. It's called Feminism and World Religions, by Arvind Sharma and Katherine K. Young, and the section on Feminism in connection with Islam makes me seethe with indignation. Especially this passage from the Qur'an about how men may treat their wives:

Men are the managers of the affairs of women because Allah has made the one superior to the other and because men spend of their wealth on women. Virtuous women are, therefore, obedient: they guard their rights carefully in their absence under the care and watch of Allah. As for those women whose defiance you have cause to fear, admonish them and keep them apart from your beds and beat them. Then, if they submit to you, do not look for excuses to punish them: note it well that there is Allah above you, Who is Supreme and Great.

Well, what is one to think? Except that this is rather on par with the Christian Old Testament Bible. The passages where little girls who were virgins were treated as spoils of war under Jehovah's direction (Moses after battle: Numbers 31: 15-18), or how Lot offered up his two virgin daughters to a mob of men instead of two men he was entertaining (Genesis 19:4-8). Nice father. However, Lot's daughters seem to bear him no grudge as later while hiding in a cave the two daughters conspired to get their father drunk so they could preserve his seed (Genesis 19: 30-38). I personally have my doubts that this preserving seed thing was really the daughter's idea. Death by stoning is also big in the Bible and is being revived by Sharia law in some parts of the world.

Modernity has modified Christianity to a certain extent. Few even diehard Christians will stand up and swear that raping little girls and killing their mothers is a good thing because the Bible said it was ordered by God, a practice that is still going on in war torn parts of the world. But Islam? Not so much modernity going on there with the Taliban. I need to talk to Bitch. For the first time since she came into my life, I deliberately go in search of her.

CHAPTER FOURTEEN
California Dreaming

I CAN'T FIND BITCH. IT'S BEEN TWO WEEKS OR MORE SINCE I've heard from her. And the weather is dreary. Cold, damp, grey...rain a little, snow a little, freeze a little, the sun peeks out a little...just a little... oh God, how I crave sunshine. And I've been sick. Sort of. A little fever, a little indigestion, a little pain in my back, but then lots of eczema on my chest and neck. And my lips are swollen. It's some kind of allergy. I have a doctor's appointment tomorrow. Marian is away on business and Hoffman is sitting on the ottoman beside me.

This cat has furniture. She has an ottoman in my office, as well as one in Marian's office. Hoffman also has a little curved plush basket on the floor downstairs in front of the fireplace and a chair that seems almost made for her. It's a small backless chair with a sling seat held to the chair by interesting leather straps. We found it in a second hand store and Hoffman immediately knew it was hers. She leaped into it as soon as it was put down on the opposite side of the fireplace. This cat is extremely far removed from the wild state. She understands both me and Marian very well and plays us off on each other.

If Marian is very busy in her office with lots of business phone calls and is focused on her work and not responding to Hoffman with loving strokes and friendly conversation Hoffman looks for me to tell her troubles to. In these suck up events she seems to be saying, "you see how I am treated by this woman who is supposed to love and protect me, she is away far too much and then when she's home, she ignores me..." At which point I will sympathize with the silly, spoiled thing and maybe offer a few morsels of her favourite treat. However, as soon as Marian concludes her phone call, Hoffman is off like a shot with her pitiful complaining cry to Marian that she feels neglected and perhaps a few more morsels of her favourite treat would sooth her ruffled feelings. Yes, Hoffman has things worked out. Would that the rest of the world was as straightforward.

The world has gone so crazy I can't believe it. Certainly not the Republican contest down south. Rick Santorum is an absolute religious fanatic, Mitt Romney a more moderate religious fanatic, and Newt Gingrich...well, not so much. Gingrich tries to pretend to be a religious too, but everybody knows he's lying. The Republican Party as a whole is trying its damndest to get abortion and even birth control back on the docket... this time through state control.

Obama is still trying to get out of Afghanistan and not be pushed into bombing Iran or letting Israel do it. Which is dicey because Netanyahu was just here a few days ago beating the war drums for an Iran invasion. What's wrong with the man? Has he no sense at all? Doesn't he know this would trigger an outright third world war? Or is he so disconnected from the rest of the world he doesn't care? But he took his fit of pique out on the Palestinians. As soon as he got home he ordered a strike to kill a Palestinian leader which in turn started four days of lobbing rockets back and forth in which twenty-seven Palestinians were killed, six of them children. His blood lust then temporarily allayed, Netanyahu agreed to a cease fire with the Palestinians.

A US soldier in Afghanistan went berserk and walked into a village and opened fire on three different homes, killing sixteen people, seven of whom were children. What's wrong with men? Let me rephrase this...what's wrong with so many men?

Today is March 24th and for the first time in weeks the sun has shone steadily all day. And I've made a momentous decision. I plan to go to California for a few months each year where I have relatives who are not born again Christians, or any kind of Christian, and just write about the physiology of women, that is, the fact that human females are the most complicated organisms that nature has ever produced, such as having three holes while men have two. The problem is, I'm not a biologist. In fact, I've never had a single biology course in any recognizable learning institution. There is no good reason I should feel compelled to write about the primacy of women as superior to anything nature has produced so far, including the males of the human species, except that nobody seems to be doing it. At least in a way that is reader friendly. I wish somebody actually qualified to do this would do it so I wouldn't have to go through the torture of recognizing how poorly qualified I am academically.

Still, Bitch has convinced me that I am not to be excused from this outlandish, onerous task so I must figure out a way to take some courses. Maybe extension courses. I've mentioned this several times to my daughters. They smile. They think I'm cute. Anyway, they've long ago given up trying to dissuade me from any project I've set my mind on.

Bitch finally wanders into my vision to give her opinion, several days after I start thinking about California. I'm clipping back the blackberry bush by the side of the house. This bush in full blossom is by far the bees' favourite. Oh, they buzz around the roses, the daises, the poppies, the bluebells but when the blackberry bush blossoms the bees go nuts. The bush will be literally covered with bees.

I am picking some berry stickers out of my gloves when I spot Bitch sitting under the camellia bush. The camellia bush can no longer be accurately described as a bush. It has grown into a tree while I wasn't looking and now leans over the stone steps where Bitch is sitting. The steps lead down to a small, recessed garden on the opposite side of the deck where I've been working on the blackberry bush. Bitch just looks at me, not saying anything. However, I can tell from the smug, smart alecky expression in her piercing dark eyes that she is pleased. And I know her pleasure concerns the news of the possibility I might go away for a bit next winter.

"So?" I ask somewhat defensively. She shrugs, pushing the owlface-shaped sunglasses that had been resting on her forehead to the top of her messy, multi coloured hair. In the bright sunlight her withered skin looks darker than usual, almost African. In fact, dressed as she is, in my old fringed skirt with an unfamiliar, scanty orange blouse that reveals her scrawny neck and shoulders I wouldn't be surprised if she got up and started dancing the bayou boogaloo.

Yes, I think, Bitch's Indian ancestors must have mated with Cajun French and both groups hid runaway slaves back in the days before the south got religion by tasting the heavy hand of the lash themselves, or at least by losing the Civil War. The Indians hid the runaway slaves because they knew the murderous hearts of conquerors first hand. And the Cajun French, too, having been expelled from Canada for not swearing allegiance to an English king,

Yes, there was sympathy there in the swamps for the runway slaves, in the hearts of these other two oppressed groups. So the miserable, frightened slaves who made it to the swamps were hidden and fed and taught how to survive in the bayous and yes, there were some genes exchanged there, too. Bitch is straight from the swamps of Louisiana and she carries all the terrors of past rapes, murders, and slaveries in her blood.

"What?" she asks, tilting her head. "Why are you glaring at me?"

"I'm not glaring," I answer. "I'm just a bit annoyed that you're so pleased that we might get out of here for a while next year. There's a lot of crazy stuff going on down there south of the border. You might not be so pleased if we actually get there."

"At least we will be in the heart of the beast," she replies. Her voice is curt, staccato. "I'm tired of fighting all of these peripheral actions, always trying to put out this fire, that tornado, these floods, the rampant forest destruction, the mutant, engineered fish and grains, gas fracking, the Enbridge pipeline, Gateway, and the truncated environmental assessment process that Stephen Harper has just brought down in his new budget. And the man simpers enough to gag a goat with the way he tries to hide his fundamental religious beliefs. It's like he thinks he belongs to some kind of secret society that makes him superior to the dummies he is supposed to be Prime Minister for. At least down south the crazy fundamentalists say they are crazy fundamentalists. They make no secret that they are waiting for the Rapture. They make no secret that they are mad."

I put my clippers down and take off my gloves. The sun is warm on my face. It's still very cool, but the first crocuses are out. I mosey over and take a seat on the bottom step of the deck, facing Bitch who is still sitting under the camellia tree. She has fallen silent.

"So?" I ask finally. "What's really on your mind?"

She looks down at her old skinny hands clasped together on her lap. She seems hesitant now. Quite unlike her. Finally she looks up and fixes me with glittering black eyes.

"We have to talk seriously about Blue Belle. About how to get rid of her."

"How can we do that?" I ask impatiently. "She has a permanent lease on her apartment. I can't just evict her. And as I'm sure you're aware, I can't physically kill her without committing suicide, and I'm not up for that."

Before Bitch can answer an idea occurs to me. "Why don't you kill her?" I ask.

"Get real. She's squatting in your territory. Only you can get rid of her."

I feel exasperated. I really would like to get rid of Blue Belle. She is preventing me from progressing as quickly as I might. And I don't have that much time left.

"Okay, how do I do that?" I ask.

"There's only one way."

"And that is?"

"You have to starve Blue Belle to death."

CHAPTER FIFTEEN
How to Get Rid of Blue Belle

"STARVE HER TO DEATH," I REPEAT, STARING AT BITCH. What on earth is she talking about? Bitch nods.

"Yes, you have to starve that little girl plumb to death. Otherwise she ain't goin' nowhere, Gramma. She'll stick to you like a duck on a June bug."

I know she is mocking me by laying on the heavy country Southern idiom and accent. I don't respond. After a moment she reaches over and picks up a thin stick off the ground. After examining the stick silently for a moment Bitch starts chewing on one side of it. This kind of thing drives me crazy. Kids chew on sticks, and dogs, even cats. Not grown-ups.

"Stop it," I order. "Put that stick down."

She turns and looks at me for a long moment. I have the fleeting impression she is going to disobey me. And if she does disobey I will have to just get up and leave. And I really do want to hear what she has to say about getting rid of Blue Belle. But no, the stick slowly slides out of her hand and falls to the ground.

"What do you mean by starving Blue Belle? I demand, feeling a little surge of relief. "She doesn't exactly eat at my table. Neither do you. I have no idea what you or Blue Belle eat. If you two eat at all. Why do you tell me such a silly thing?"

Black eyes flash over my face in exasperation.

"If you would think for a moment you would understand what I'm talking about. You know neither Blue Belle nor I eat human food. We exist on ideas, beliefs, emotions, memories, both personal memories and race memories."

Her voice is full of passion. The passion that scares me at times. During our conversation we have become seated side by side on the edge of the brick walkway. I move away a fraction.

"Okay, so how do you suppose I go about starving that kind of cosmic conflagration?" I ask, but I think I already know what she means. And Bitch knows that I know. She stands up and brushes bits of bark from the stick she was chewing on from her ridiculous skirt. I notice she is barefoot. It's too cold yet to be going about barefoot. And then I become aware that I am barefoot, too. I've left my shoes and socks at the bottom of the deck stairs.

"You have to stop answering when she appears and wants to talk, and you have to stop inviting her to see those silly movies with you," Bitch goes on in a flat, commanding voice.

"They're not silly..." I begin. And then stop. They are silly.

"You know they're silly. And every time you watch one, especially with Blue Belle, you dig the bog deeper that you're trying to crawl out of. The bog that women everywhere are trying to climb out of...the religious quicksand that will suck you right back in given half a chance. You know why? Your brain remembers. Your brain remembers all the times you felt pleasure being in church, a joy even; there was an emotional community there and you felt safe. You haven't felt safe since you left the church, and revisiting that safety with Blue Belle makes you long for it again."

I look up at Bitch.

"It's harmless enough..." I begin, searching for a good defence. But there isn't any. I know very well that she is telling the truth.

"You have to start on this soon," Bitch continues, ignoring my faint protest. "You don't have time to dither."

"But I'm a mother," I plead. "How can I do this? How can I just ignore her until she shrivels up? Blue Belle is like a little girl..."

"And you can no longer allow her to hold you back. Your love for your sons kept you from progressing for many years. I worried a lot during those years when you were sorting out your personal love for your sons and your ability to consider men in the collective. It was dicey, but you got through it okay. A lot of women bog down at that point and give it all up. But you didn't. You faced the dilemma. And you have been able to articulate to other women that while it is true that the personal is political it is also true that women give birth to sons as well as daughters and women can love men in private but also struggle with the male collective. This thing with Blue Belle may be even trickier for you because you associate her with your mother and your own young self. But you're not young anymore. And your mother died on your seventieth birthday. That was thirteen years ago. You're a very old woman yourself, now. You have to let Blue Belle go."

I get up and collect my shoes and socks, leaving Bitch standing there. I can feel her brooding black eyes still on my back as I go into the house.

I feel sick and heavy hearted. I find myself weeping a bit as I brush up the kitchen before Marian gets home. But it'll be okay. March 18 is Sue's birthday. My fourth child and first daughter. Hopefully she will be able to come to us from Vancouver for a couple of days. The thought cheers me.

CHAPTER SIXTEEN
Our Ancient Mothers and the Shock Doctrine

GAIA MOVES IN MYSTERIOUS WAYS HER WONDERS TO perform. Or her catastrophes, of course. One often doesn't know the difference between the two until sometime down the road. Today is a down the road day. It is also May the first. Almost two months since Bitch and I had our talk in the garden about starving Blue Belle. But I haven't put Bitch's dictates into action yet concerning Blue Belle. I keep putting it off. Besides, I have a lot of other stuff to think about.

Marian advised me last week that her counter offer on the house was accepted. The inspector is here today inspecting the house from top to bottom. It makes me nervous. He is up in the attic. What is he finding up there? Not enough insulation? Nesting animals? And he was down in the basement. What was he looking for in that space? Weak underpinning that may portend that the house could just collapse any moment? I don't like this kind of tension. We have to leave at one o'clock because the woman who is buying is coming to speak to the inspector along with the real estate agent.

And I am very worried about my daughter Sue. She has another aneurysm. Smaller this time and not close to the bursting point as the first one was eight years ago by the time it was discovered But this one has to be fixed soon. And will be. Sue will be operated on next week on the 9th. Marian will be going down to be with her. Sue doesn't want me to come. She thinks I get too anxious and this makes her anxious. I don't know what to do about this. I try not to show my anxiety when one of my children falls ill but

I've already lost two. Give me a break. Any mother would have heightened anxiety over a child having a brain aneurysm. That's the brain, for heaven's sake. They are going to be messing around with my daughter's brain.

It is now May 11, the operation is over and Sue is already back home. Marian is with her during the day and Rhodes will be there at night in case she needs anything. The operation was on Wednesday and it is only late Friday. Sue has all of her senses intact and is walking about. I just talked to her on the phone. With all my anger at western medicine's treatment of women, I am happy my daughter had a good surgeon. A man, too. What can I say? Do men make better brain surgeons than women? Who knows as of yet? There aren't enough women brain surgeons to find out. But I give thanks humbly for Canada's health care system. Yes, Canada's public universal health care system is wonderful. I damn the conservatives and banks and investment houses and stock markets and Fraser Institute and the BC Liberal Party and the Harper government for trying to turn Canada's public health care into a private system.

The house has sold. We must be out by the second of July. Packing looms. What to take? And where am I going? For the immediate future I'm not going anywhere except two blocks over to my daughter Margaret's house. However, as she and her husband of twenty-two years have separated for good I can be of help to her until she sells her house. But before I leave this house, I must think about Blue Belle. Margaret's house is considerably smaller than the one I am moving out of. Blue Belle will likely do a lot of complaining. I know I must think seriously about getting rid of her. I need to clear my decks in order to think clearly about the new book I am already making notes for, which will be in part about religion, and what religion has done to women. And I can't wait much longer to get started.

But still I procrastinate. To stall off serious thinking about Blue Belle I busy myself with packing. And Marian brought a movie home this evening from the village that I had to view. It's called Make a Joyful Noise, starring Dolly Parton and Queen Latifah. Marian knows my musical tastes. Lots of gospel music and great singing. And of course I had to invite Blue Belle. She and I both enjoyed the movie immensely. Blue Belle wanted to see parts of it again. I firmly objected and she reluctantly went to her own quarters. This morning I am ready to get to work on the packing.

I start in the office. All the papers! And books, more books. Case law in large binders. Voluminous copies of court transcripts. Paper histories of four different blockades I was involved in; Clayoquot Sound, the Elaho, the Walbran Valley, and the last one at Eagleridge Bluffs. In one of the Eagleridge Bluff binders I find two great photos of Harriet Nahanee. In one photo Harriet is holding the Mohawk flag; in another she is reading a copy of the Royal Proclamation of 1763 to police officers while I stand beside her. "Oh, Harriet, I hope you are at peace," I whisper. "You came to symbolize something dear to me."

That something dear...was a rock hard stubborn woman who refused to call an outrage against women and children and the earth a good thing, or recognize these outrages as necessities. Even when almost everyone in her band and council and her family and on her reserve said she was wrong, and warned they wouldn't have anything to do with her if she persisted in her actions, and she would become a pariah among her people. And she did become a pariah in her community. As did I, fifty years before, in Louisiana, during school integration struggles in the sixties. And again, many years later, when I returned to Ucluelet, a logging community at the time, after being released from prison for blockading logging trucks in Clayoquot Sound. But the first time was the hardest. I still bear scars from that one.

Some of the schools in Baton Rouge were threatening to close rather than allow black kids to go to school with white kids. I joined a small group of white parents who went down to our local elementary public school where my children attended and picketed outside the school demanding the school stay open and integrate peacefully. I became an instant pariah in my own neighbourhood. I walked out of my church after the pastor refused to endorse peaceful integration and have never been back to a Christian Church. Childhood friends cut me on the street and my sons were questioned in school. Oh, yes. I received some death threats and there was garbage dumped on our lawn on a regular basis.

My father, who preached across the river in a country church, felt I was putting myself and the children in danger. So did my mother. They didn't exactly disagree with my opposition to school closings, only felt that putting myself and the kids in danger was wrong. The rest were hopeless. My only real supporter was my husband John. And while we went our separate ways years later after immigrating to Canada I will always remember that time when he was so kind to me when the rest of the world seemed so cruel.

So I understood Harriet Nahanee very well when I learned of her situation on her home base. I knew the courage she must muster every day when she went back home to her reserve from the blockade. The reserve where the chiefs and council had bargained away the Squamish Nation's claim to Eagleridge Bluffs and given it over to the provincial government. Harriet was fighting not only my chiefs and councils; she was in addition fighting the ones she lived with. The others could not know the enormous courage this took. I saluted her. She was my comrade in arms in a deep, emotional sense. But while she was a feminist, she didn't interpret the Stockholm syndrome through a feminist lens. For her the Stockholm syndrome was a graphic illustration of the historical defeat of the indigenous Indians of the Americas. And the Proclamation of 1763 was still the light under which Indians could claim sovereignty and be free of foreign molestation on their own lands.

Madame Justice B. Brown wouldn't even allow Harriet to read the Royal Proclamation in court. She wouldn't allow Harriet to say much of anything. She convicted Harriet of criminal contempt of court, sentenced her to 14 days in jail, and Harriet died not quite a week after release. And she has left me this damned Stockholm syndrome to wrestle with.

So I've been packing. Two copies of the Syndrome.

But first, I decide to take a nap. And while napping I have a dream. I hate it when other writers start detailing their dreams. Dreams are so boring to people who have to listen to them. Of course everybody's own dreams are absolutely fascinating. Or scary. Or both. My nap dream was so odd I had to lie still and solidify it in my head before moving. It was about the two cats my daughter Rose Mary had years ago when she lived in Arizona with her young son and husband and I was visiting. She had named these two multi-colored female cats, Bo and Willow.

The cats were themselves litter mates and they bore their own litters on the same day with their first pregnancies. Rose Mary gave the mama cats each a big cardboard box in the large, airy basement for their own individual kittens. Each box was lined with comfy torn up blankets so all were cozy. But the following day the mama cats had rearranged things. They were all, cats and kittens, in Willow's box. The box wasn't built to accommodate such an extended family so Rose Mary took Bo and Bo's kittens back to their own house. But by the next day all felines, both mamas and babies, were back in Willow's box.

At this point Rose Mary just cut out one side of the boxes and put them together which gave enough room for everyone and this arrangement seemed to satisfy all concerned. But then Rose Mary noticed something else that seemed odd to her. Bo wasn't as maternal as Willow for whatever reason, and Willow seemed to be doing most of the nursing for all of the kittens. Sometimes Bo would leave the entire bunch and stay away for hours. However, she always returned and offered up her own nursing apparatus for the group of kittens so Bo could take a break.

Whatever the arrangement was between the two, the kittens seemed to thrive. They were healthy, happy balls of fluff and after weaning Rose Mary tied bright red bows round their necks, put them in a large wicker basket with a "for free" sign and sat them down in front of the largest grocery store in Tucson on a little folding table.

I stood guard with Rose Mary. We only had to intervene once...when a rambunctious little 3 year boy tried to pick one of the kittens up by his hind legs. We convinced the mother of the boy that her son was too young for such a small kitten and even with that distraction, and extracting promises to neuter from all of the new owners, the entire operation was completed in an hour. Both Bo and Willow, now neutered themselves, also found new homes with a little help from their friends.

However, the maternal behavior of Bo and Willow and the way they had shared kitten nursing duties stayed in the back of my mind. I didn't know exactly where to put this example of feline cooperation. But when I woke up from my nap dream of Bo and Willow and the kittens there was another image beside it...another one that had plagued me for years because I couldn't understand the meaning of it.

It was an image of a woman with three breasts. I had seen a photograph of this somewhere. The third breast appeared normal and was placed directly under the woman's right breast. As the day waned the image of the three breasted woman was still there, flitting around the edges of my mind. After dinner I sat down at the computer to see what I could find. What I found was interesting.

There's something called the nipple line that extends from the armpit down to the bottom of the last rib where it has been known in rare instances, very rare instances, for a third nipple to appear. Sometimes the nipple would only be in the form of a mole, or something that looks like a mole. How weird. I had just had a rather large mole taken off that was situated right under my right breast on the nipple line. The things one learns from Google. I surveyed the information below:

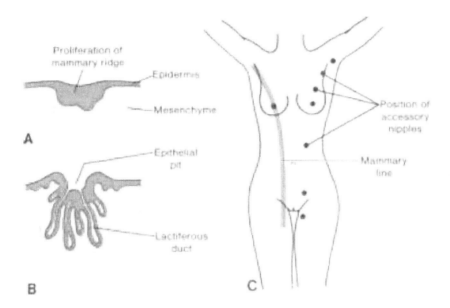

CLINICAL CORRELATES Mammary Gland Abnormalities

Polythelia is a condition where accessory nipples have formed due to the persistence of fragments of the mammary line (Fig. 18.4C). Accessory nipples may develop anywhere along the original mammary line, but usually appear in the axillary region.

Polymastia occurs when a remnant of the mammary line develops into a complete breast.

Interesting. And weird. The information and diagram rather suggests that at one time female humans, or the evolutionary line that became human, many have had more than just two breasts.

In my reading, from time to time, I find discussions concerning the curious phenomenon of how women of reproductive age who live together for any length of time will begin to have their menses around the same time each month. I've wondered about this because nobody, including scientists, seems to be able to find a good explanation for the phenomenon. It is generally accepted that in all species Mother Nature seems to try to give gifts that enhance the chances of each species survival. But how does species survival compute with cohabiting human women having their monthly periods at the same time? What benefit would this bring to the human species?

Especially when the prevailing propaganda is that most women suffer from something called the premenstrual syndrome which our society (male) swears up and down exists and insists that women are universally bitchy and uncooperative during their periods. If this is indeed true, then how could it possibly be good for the human race to have so many women the world over who do live together in groups supposedly experiencing massive bitchiness and irritability at the same time? And how have the menstruating women, under the biological pressure of being out of emotional control during it all, according to the many learned medical opinions (male) managed to keep from killing each other?

It's a puzzle. Nobody has figured it out yet that I know of. Either most of the premenstrual syndrome talk is just that, talk, because Mother Nature does not make silly mistakes like having cohabiting women crabby all at the same time, or that the talk of such a syndrome either accidentally or by design, obscures something very fundamental to the survival of the human race.

Like what, you may ask? I think it may be like scientists have been asking the wrong questions about why women's periods become synchronized in the first place. Instead of asking why women tend to synchronize their periods under certain circumstances, the better question would be why do women synchronize their ovulation periods. After all, bleeding only occurs after ovulation in healthy, unfertilized women which means that many menstruating women of our earliest ancestors were also ovulating at roughly the same times. And when the question of synchronized ovulation is the focus instead of synchronized menstruation then both, and the questions surrounding them, begin to make sense.

In the early days of human hunting and gathering, we are told by many anthropologists, men did not contribute to the feeding of children, or of the women, for that matter. The feeding of children was entirely the purview of women. So we have small groups of humans, according to the anthropologists, where the women and children lived in a kind of communal grouping close to but apart from the men. Again, what would it benefit humans as a whole for a number or numbers of women to have babies at roughly the same time?

Dr.Leonard Shlain (Chief of Laparoscopic surgery a California-Pacific Center in San Francisco) in his book, Sex, Time and Power, points out that human mothers are at a terrible disadvantage compared to most other mammals when giving birth, primarily because of the size of the human infant's head (I disagree with most of Dr. Shlain's theories on sexual evolution but I go with this one). As human infants' heads grew larger over evolutionary time it seems that human mothers' ability to accommodate these large heads through the human birth canal became a dicey business. And Dr. Shlain quotes Dr. Peter Ellison (Dept. of Human Evolution of Biology at Harvard): "The ninety-six hours or so following the onset of parturition (birth contractions) constitute the greatest period of mortality risk that a typical human will ever face."

In the past, many women died along with their babies during these ninety-six hours of parturition. Even during my own mother's day, it wasn't unusual for women to die in childbirth. Sometimes the infants died along with their mothers, but sometimes they lived. And in the birthing of our ancient mothers (hunters and gathers) some infants may have been successfully delivered before their mothers died and would have survived if given the milk of other nursing mothers. And if this did indeed happen relatively frequently, then it would have become very important in evolutionary terms, and for the survival of the human race, that there be enough other nursing mothers on hand who could feed extra babies along with their own infants.

But aside from the need of feeding orphan babies, there would be other reasons a woman might not be able to breast feed even if she survived the birthing process. Some mothers may have been too wounded by child birth to breast feed, or suffered an accident or illness prior or after birthing, or been the victim of a wild animal attack.

We know that a mother's milk production increases in relation to how much she nurses an infant or infants. But even if in a given year all mothers and babies in a group had survived, and were well, perhaps it would also have been a great advantage for the survival of the group as a whole (in early hunting and gathering remember that men did not feed women or children) if several of the mothers could go out for the day food gathering, knowing that their babies would be well nursed by the other mothers while they were away.

These early mothers must have worked in close cooperation with each other and the older women, or the human race would not have survived. And it was this gift of group female biology that allowed women to form bonds of mutual support for the survival of the young, to share the milk and honey that enabled humans to multiply and spread out over the earth. And this female capacity for care and empathy keeps the world glued together today.

"And don't forget to bring in estrus," Bitch says, hovering over my shoulder.

I stop writing and look up at her.

"What about estrus?" I ask, annoyed. She is interrupting my train of thought.

"Well, you know...all those writers and researchers, they can't figure out what happened to women's estrus. Women are mammals; right...all the other mammals have estrus. Their females don't have to bother looking pretty all the time. Their dates come around regular as clockwork agitated by a certain scent or colour, like that Dr. Shlain says in his book. And the females are not bothered with the bums at other times."

"Yes, so? So you think you know what happened to the human female estrus?" I inquire politely, quickly recalling a sarcastic tone.

"Of course. Nothing happened to it. It's still there. It's just hidden, that's all, because women are separated. When women come together in groups for any extended period of time their estrus works just fine. In the raw state of nature women nursed their babies from four to six years and during this time they didn't ovulate. And nursing decreases libido. Only when their menses started again after weaning did the women know they were ready to mate again. A different guy this time if they could even remember who the previous guy was as there were probably a few of them before she got pregnant. A bitch in heat is a bitch in heat."

She laughed but I didn't think her remark was at all funny. I hate references to women as bitches although that is what I call the crazy woman sneering at my elbow.

But that conversation took place when Marian and I (and of course Blue Belle and Bitch) were still living in Merryland in the big house with Hoffman the cat. Before the family decision to sell the house.

I am at the moment, this moment being the 5th of July, 2012, at two-thirty p.m., staying with my daughter Margaret in her house. I will be here until the little nondescript condo where I will be living in for the foreseeable future is ready. I expect to move in by the first week in September. Margaret, now a single working woman, is out of the house quite smartly in the mornings and doesn't return until after five. And Margaret's cat, Kitty Brown, has accepted me as a source of possible extra Kitty treats and a lap to mull things over on when his main person isn't dispensing the required amount of attentiveness he requires. But he's a great, beautiful tawny colored cat, almost like a miniature lion. We get on.

Kitty Brown was lying on my lap when the news came on the radio about the discovery of the God particle. I moved the cat off my lap and crossed the room to turn up the volume on the radio. Kitty Brown, disturbed by the disruption of his tranquil sprawl across my lap, stalked off, his plumy tail swishing indignantly. He didn't want to hear about the God particle. I let him out and then returned to my seat on the couch. And found Blue Belle sitting there, too, waiting for me. I wasn't surprised. It was time she made an appearance. And at any mention of God and Blue Belle is there, ready to testify.

"Blue Belle, I really don't think this is anything that will interest you," I said, wanting to hear the report in peace. "It's scientific. It has something to do with the Big Bang theory, you know, how the universe was first created."

She sniffed. I hate Blue Belle's delicate sniffs worse than anything. They are just so dismissive, so superior.

"All those scientists would have to do is read the Bible and they would know how the universe was first created," she said in that familiar sanctimonious tone that grates like sand paper across my nerve endings.

I couldn't stand it. I really wanted to hear this report and to try to understand as much of it as I possibly can.

"Blue Belle, please go to your room," I said crossly. "Or go somewhere. The sun is shining and there are roses growing outside."

To my surprise she didn't argue or get angry. She rose slowly, with a barely perceptible martyr's sigh. But no, she wasn't going to leave without a parting shot.

"Betty, please look at me," she said firmly. There was something in the tone of her request that gave me pause. I looked up at her, waiting. For some reason, in that moment she seemed older than usual and it struck me there weren't quite so many flounces fluffing out from her pale blue skirt and petticoat.

"What do you want?" I asked impatiently.

"I want you to know that I've been around for a long time. And I'm not going anywhere. At least nowhere that I can't find you."

She sounded so serious. And determined. Would the woman prove to be some kind of super stalker, I wondered as I stared after her retreating figure? But it doesn't matter, I told myself firmly, turning my attention back to the news of the God particle. After all, Blue Belle lives in my house. I can evict her anytime. And if she won't go willingly, well, there is this other option. But right now, dang gum it, I want to hear about the so called God Particle.

Too late. The brief interview with the scientist talking about the God particle is over. How in the world are ordinary citizens supposed to make sense of this kind of brief announcement? It's maddening. The rest of the news is about the struggle going on in Syria.

Funny, the violence in Syria all seemed relatively straight forward several days ago. Hillary Clinton in her righteous anger stance against Assad, the president of Syria, cut a formidable figure. However, the protesters, the ones doing the fighting against the regime in Syria, seem to be infiltrated by the Muslim Brotherhood with ties to Al Qaeda. Why did this not alarm the media? It alarmed me. But this point was ignored by the western press, or lightly slid over, including programs like Democracy Now. But I have just finished reading Naomi Klein's book The Shock Doctrine.

I'm in a bit of shock after digesting Klein's illuminating book. And absolutely sure that we Canadians are not getting the straight news from any of our main news sources and that includes the CBC. According to Klein's thesis (and we can back check the news sources ourselves and find that what she says is true) the US deliberately plunges into any country that is experiencing some measure of difficulty in order to take advantage of its resources or geography. Or even if a targeted country is not experiencing any particular difficulty at a particular moment the US will provoke one. However, the favourite time for some kind of US intervention or outright invasion is when other countries are trying to deal with wars, terrorist attacks or natural disasters.

At the moment, in my opinion, the US is desirous of crippling Syria with regime change so they can move in closer to Iran and also continue to encircle China. The US would love to invade Syria, as would Israel, but China and Russia won't let them. Even though the US is supposed to be fighting Al Qaeda and terrorism, and the opposition is composed of the Muslim Brotherhood with ties to Al Qaeda, the US is gung-ho to back the opposition. I think the CIA and Obama administration consider the Muslim Brotherhood, even with their ties to Al Qaeda (this is supposed to be where the US war on terror is directed) are after all, while dangerous, are ignorant. And therefore controllable. At least until the US can get their gear into the country and occupy it.

The US would then be able to treat Syria as they have treated Iraq, Libya, and Afghanistan. And typically, they are also at the moment, supporting the reinstatement of a longtime dictator in the Maldives. Mohamed Nasheed, also known as The Island President, is famous for bringing democracy to his country and fighting hard to bring environmental protection to his country since his election in 2008. But this was just too much for the US. They don't like democracy in the Maldives, or anywhere else where they covet territory for their use, or oil, or other minerals, including gold and diamonds. But as the Maldives have none of these, the US wants to use the country for strategic purposes. So the US is supporting the return of Naumoon Abdul Gayoom, a corrupt long-time dictator who tortured Nasheed and kept him in solitary confinement for months because he opposed the dictator.

The Obama administration, for all its sickening talk about democracy and the separation of church and state and the rights of women, could care less that Mohamed Nasheed brought a secular state to the Maldives and that their chosen boy Gayoom is pressing for an Islamic state. With Sharia law. Obama evidently sees no contraindication in his policies. I get so frustrated when I hear Obama referred to as a black president. The man is half white. I don't think he even recognizes his black half anymore, much less deigns to consult it.

And it seems there are billions to be made by gold plated US citizens in protecting the right foreign dictators. Massive physical constructs have to be built to provide for the deployment of troops. Troops have to be housed, fed and entertained. Structures have to be built for surveillance, communication, for port facilities, air fields and nobody knows how much money for lawyers to represent the number of troops who will be charged with rape of local women. Female US soldiers may or may not have anybody to represent them on the same charges.

Halliburton will make more billions along with other corporations who lie in Obama's bosom of favoritism. Just as US bombs have blown existing structures apart in other countries, it will be US construction firms that half ass rebuild what they blow apart. Oh, how they all wish they could go into Syria and get to work on finishing tearing down what hasn't been bombed out by the Syrian government or bombed in and up by the Muslim Brotherhood.

However, today is July 28th and while the fighting is going on something fierce in Syria, I haven't heard anything the last couple of days about Hillary Clinton calling for Assad to step down. I think China has sent a message. To Obama. And I think the crux of it goes like this:

> Friend, if you are a friend and want to remain a friend, I suggest you stop talking about regime change and sending in military assistance to the opposition in Syria. We know you. We know what you're up to. And you had better recognize what you would be up against if you try to invade Syria to get a foothold in Iran. Or to invade Syria for any reason, including your wish to make billions reconstructing what you have already destroyed as in Iraq and Libya. Are you forgetting who owns you? Who owns your debt? Who can cash in all those bonds and refuse to buy more? Get a grip, friend. Now

Well, at least Hillary Clinton has shut up about Assad killing his own people as though the opposition is not also killing their own people and are we to believe that in a civil war that is not what both sides set out to do?

Kill their own people? The ones who don't agree with them? Would it be better for the US troops who are foreigners to come in and kill the people? To kill the people to stop the people from killing their own people? To wipe out a village with bombing by foreigners to free the villagers who are left to sign up for democracy? And is that what the Afghan mothers are reported to have threatened their naughty children with: be good, or else democracy will come and get you?

Immediately after the news this morning, I turned on Margaret's computer to answer emails. Only I couldn't concentrate. My mind was still on the other news story of the day. It seems that our Premier of British Columbia, Christy Clark, has told Alberta's premier, Alison Redford, that she (Redford) couldn't build the Enbridge Northern Gateway Pipeline across BC without adequate compensation for British Columbia.

That's what our premier was worried about...adequate compensation. Not that the pipeline was evil in itself, Christy Clark wasn't talking about all the things wrong with the proposed pipeline, only that her province wanted adequate compensation for the privilege of being debauched by dirty oil and dirty trade. We say dirty oil because the sticky tar stuff has to be blasted out of the sand that contains it, with water. Any woman (or man) who has ever tried to wash oily tar out of work pants or anything similar, can imagine how much water it would take to blast sand out of tar. And this isn't grey water, it is poisoned water. It can't be used again. This water is lost to us forever. It is lost forever to the total amount of water on the earth.

And we say dirty trade because the bitumen (tar sands sludge) will eventually spill both at home and in sea lanes. The other fearless provincial leader Alison Redford of Alberta and the tarsands, says no, we will not share revenue with you, Christy. I will only pay you a little bit for violating your body with my dirt and if you don't like it you can lump it because I can force you to. I have the law and precedent on my side. Our situations are unequal, see? You're the prostitute, I'm the John. I'm the man, you're the woman.

Will fearless Christy back down? She doesn't have to. The federal government is the police and they know she is only bluffing, that she is just putting up a brave warrior woman front for votes. If she would stand up and say that for no amount of money would she allow Alberta's tarsands bitumen to pour though the lands of BC I would stand up and cheer. No, I wouldn't do that. I wouldn't be able to. I would be in a dead faint on the floor, gasping for air. But in other news...

India is still in the midst of a black out in many major populations centers with accompanying issues of gummed up transportation and water systems. There is a break out of the Ebola virus in Gambia that is scary as hell and the civil war in Syria rages on. But all media attention is on the Olympics.

Two days ago Ye Shiwen, a sixteen year old Chinese girl broke the world's record for swimming by winning gold in in the 400m individual medley at the London Olympics. The US coaches, astonished at the young girl's time, immediately brought up the suspicion that she was doping. The accusation spread, and seemed to stem from resentment, because she broke the time of Ryan Lochte, who took gold for the men's medley. This remarkable event was evidently too remarkable for some of the US coaches, who suggested that the girl had to be doping. However, her tests came back clean. She also passed her doping tests on her second gold swimming medal a few days later. While the Olympic Committee has supported Ye Shiwen and said her feats should be celebrated there is still no apology from the US coach or any US authority. And a curious thing...there was no mention of either Ye Shiwen's remarkable feats or the voiced suspicions of the US on CBC radio. In fact, CBC was so silent on this extraordinary happening that I might think I had dreamed the entire episode were it not for the reporting from BBC and Al Jazeera online.

Several days later: when Margaret came home from her shop we went out to the thrift stores to try to find a tall reading lamp to use as a base for her home made mannequin. When finished she plans to sew an outfit for the mannequin and display it in her shop to advertise to her customers that she is also a dress maker. The mannequin isn't finished yet, but the hard part is over. That involved finding a garment snug enough to fit Margaret's torso from her neck just to below her hips without cutting off the blood circulation, a huge roll of strapping tape, a how to DVD, and most of the afternoon. The idea was to wrap the strapping tape in strategically placed strips on the torso until the wrapped subject looked very like a mummy and then cut the whole thing up the back and slip the contraption off. To my amazement it worked beautifully. Now the mannequin just has to be stuffed, secured to a base and she is ready for dressing. We haven't yet found a floor lamp to Margaret's liking. Just before bed that night she called me into the front room to take advantage of the large windows in order to gaze at the moon. A big fat round delicious looking moon.

"It's so strange," Margaret murmured, her voice all soft with wonder. "You know, we are just small creatures here on a big ball of earth and there's a big ball of a moon up there and the sun is a big round ball, too..."

"I know," I replied, adopting her same awe struck tone. "It's weird just being alive. I've often thought about how weird being alive actually is... Because evolution did all this unimaginable stuff and then gave us the consciousness to realize how very weird it all is, I mean, Kitty Brown doesn't look at the moon and wonder about evolution."

"No, and speaking of Kitty Brown, he's still outside. It's time for him to come in."

Margaret went to find her cat but I stayed at the window, staring at the moon and thinking of the power of the universe and how paradoxical it is that our earth and everything on it is so fragile, yet so magnificent, and that our minds cannot really comprehend the complexity of why the moon and sun and earth are round. Like eggs. Like a woman's eggs. More or less. Eerie. You would think that the common shape of these important entities would be noted more by scientists. Scientists other than Dr. Natalie Angier, who in her best-selling book, Woman, does wax poetic about the human egg.

But it is now August 22. Blue Belle and Bitch both pay me fewer visits. I don't know why. Perhaps the ghost of Mary Daly has given them pause. I have gone from reading Daly's book, Beyond God the Father, to studying it. Or maybe the lack of visits from my inner residents is because I am more concerned right now about getting the little condo I will be moving into habitable, so I can get my office back together, and this doesn't threaten either one. But I have spoken too soon. Bitch has just sauntered into my space. I think I know already what she wants to talk about. Illegitimate rape.

CHAPTER SEVENTEEN
Blue Belle Falls III

RAPE ENRAGES BITCH. AND THE CRAZINESS OF THE RECENT pronouncement from a US politician, that there are actually two different kinds of rape, "legitimate" and "illegitimate," is brain numbing. This claim was made by Todd Akin, Republican Representative of Missouri. He claimed that in an illegitimate rape, that is a rape that a woman really didn't want, the woman's body has the power to shut the whole thing down (that is, prevent the rapist's sperm from travelling from her vagina to her fallopian tubes). Therefore, the fact that a woman or girl got pregnant from a rape means that she actually enjoyed the rape because her body "didn't automatically shut the whole thing down."

Bitch's eyes glitter with a murderous rage. I suffer through her tirade without comment. Todd Akin, the man who said such a thing and seems to believe it, is too stupid and ignorant to risk popping a blood vessel over. Surely the American people, who will be voting in the US election, both men and women, will realize how ignorant and stupid Mr. Akin is. But how can I depend on it? I can remember not terribly long ago, a respectable southern gentleman explaining to me why there wasn't such a thing as actual rape. He held his index finger over the opening of a vinegar cruet on the table of an upscale restaurant where we were dining and tried to stick his finger into the opening of the cruet while moving the bottle around with his other hand.

"See?" he said triumphantly. "All the woman has to do is keep moving that opening around if she doesn't want it."

I stared at this gentleman in disbelief. He was a respectable business-man and was wearing an expensive suit and tie, for God's sake. Okay, yes, we were in Louisiana and he was a true native son. But was he really that ignorant, I wondered? Perhaps he was. I suddenly remembered that I had a very important meeting to attend and I was late. A man this ignorant was dangerous to be in the company of any woman, young, old, or in-between. Still, in remembering this incident, I wonder if perhaps we have all become so stunted by our culture ~ Canadian as well as American ~ that we have trouble recognizing when a person in public office has limited intelligence. But in the days that immediately follow Bitch's outburst, I become increasingly preoccupied with my big move to my own little nondescript condo.

And the move is now complete. I am living alone again, an old woman on her own. I have to say it's a relief although I will miss daily contact with Marian, Rhodes and Margaret. Still, I like having my days ordered to my own specification. And Margaret, having sold her house and in the process of dividing proceeds with her husband, is looking for a condo for herself around the same area where I am living.

We are approaching the middle of November and the weather remains warm. There is the usual worry about forest fires. The farmers are suffering from lack of rain on the Prairies. And there is unbelievable barbarism in the middle East. A fourteen-year-old girl in Pakistan was deliberately shot in the neck and head by the Taliban because she attended a school and wants to be a doctor.

This is so outrageous. The misogyny of the radical Islamists is beyond belief. I wrote furiously in my blog, even without the urging of Bitch, trying to dispel some of the sorrow in my heart at this turn of events and looking desperately for bright spots. I did find a few. And so I wrote:

Taliban and the Rising Tide of Women

Two women have captured my heart in the last few days, Malala Yousafzai in Pakistan and the Australian Prime Minister Julia Gillard. I'm sure that most of you have heard about Malala. She is only fourteen years old. She lies in a medically-induced coma trying to survive gunshot wounds to the head and neck. She was shot point blank by the Taliban because she attended school and spoke out for the rights of other girls to attend school. If she lives, the Taliban has promised to try to murder her again. The bright spot in this, if there is one, is that Malala's family is supporting her and her actions against the murderous threats of the Taliban.

Another bright spot occurred in the Australian parliament recently. Prime Minister Julia Gillard gave the most passionate speech condemning misogyny in government I have ever heard. Check out Gillard's speech attacking Tony Abbott (opposition) for his sexist actions and remarks in government on Youtube if you haven't already. Julia Gillard is spell binding. The video has gone viral.

BC MP Elizabeth May and Premier Pauline Marois of Quebec are two Canadian women leaders trying to move governments to embrace a more egalitarian value system. Their efforts to increase respect for women, kids and the environment are of course severely hampered by our prime minister who belongs to a Christian evangelical fundamentalist church. The pastor and congregation of this church are heavily steeped in Biblical prophecy which they take literally. In my view this in turn fosters the belief that it doesn't matter much about the environment anyway, or the needs of the poor, who are primarily women and children because it's all going to end soon as we are in the End Times. According to scripture the End Times precedes the Second Coming of Christ.

Mary Daly, international Catholic theologian, Philosopher and feminist (she died two years ago) suggested in her book "Beyond God the Father" that the Second Coming so anticipated by Christian fundamentalists might be a huge surprise when it gets here. Daly suggests the Second Coming is really the "Be-Coming" of women in leadership roles demanding equality for all humans along with care for the environment. In other words, Daly thinks women will bring the end of patriarchy. In the meantime we have male Conservative politicians who are trying to bring back the debate on when life begins, which is of course, the angle they hope might eventually outlaw abortion. The question of when life begins for a single human egg is still fuzzy, but one thing is becoming clearer all the time, and that is how, when and where the first truly human person (Homo sapiens sapiens) was born.

Homo means man, of course, and Homo sapiens sapiens means thinking man (to differentiate modern humans from Neanderthal types). When these words are strung together they mean the human man, hence the term mankind. Women are supposed to be included in this description. The thought and image of women as subordinate to the male simply became part of religious thinking which eventually turned into *civil law in Europe. Remember Adam and Eve? This myth is deeply embedded in at least half of the world's brains, both male and female. But the entire world is going to have to rethink this Biblical myth, and other creation stories, because according to the geneticists at University of California, Berkeley, when Eve was born there was no Adam.*

The very first Homo sapiens sapiens wasn't a guy at all...she was a baby girl. And she was a mutant, so to speak. That is, she mutated in her mother's womb to become the first truly human being, one that differentiated her from all the other man-apes (and women-apes). According to these geneticists this happened approximately two hundred thousand years ago in Africa and all of the humans on earth today are descended from this first human female child. But after the rise of patriarchy female children were treated brutally as property of the men; this is still happening in many countries. Let us centre our minds and hearts on the life and death struggle our little sister and daughter Malala Yousafzai is waging. More later about how and when the geneticists made this discovery of the first human

I've already received some flack about this from a Canadian journalist who suggests that Julia Gillard, Australian prime minister, is no feminist. He relies on John Pilger, an Australian journalist, to discredit Gillard's credentials as a feminist. I'll have to do more research on her: we'll see. Malala Yousafzai has been flown to England for medical treatment and is holding her own. I have just finished reading an email from Stone Iwassa that includes an update on the Mohawk nine points being undertaking to turn the rule of male dominance over to their traditional Mohawk Matrilineal Authority. Maybe they can give us some guidance on this.

It is Oct. 27th[th] and there is a tentative drizzle outside. There is a huge storm plowing through Haiti, headed to the east coast of the US and Canada. I have yet to turn on the heat in my little condo although today is a bit chilly. I begin to unpack more of the videos and CD's I brought with me, and am sorting through Gospel, Country, and Pop albums. This is an exhausting task as the albums bring back so many memories. It's too much. I decide to take an early break with a peanut butter and jelly sandwich. The book I pick up to accompany my munching is Beyond God the Father, by Mary Daly. Daly is into something called "psychic androgyny."

I'm not sure I get it. I kind of do. But not really. It isn't clear enough. Daly's theory on psychic androgyny seems to offer, as an answer to the problem of male violence, the possibility that there is the potential for men to become more like women and for women to also change and incorporate some masculine attributes, and because the female has borne the burden of reproduction of the species and has survived the oppression of men, they have the compassion and the patience to lead in the transformation that will become the psychic androgyny of the human species.

I don't know about this. But I haven't time for "studying for a spell" as my mother used to call mulling something over. Back to sorting the CDs. Songs by the Blind Boys of Alabama. I haven't played the disk in a long time. Blue Belle used to love it. It occurs to me that I haven't seen Blue Belle since we moved into the condo. And a couple of weeks before that, even. And I guess I haven't invited her, for that matter. Subconsciously I have been ignoring her. I begin to wander through my inner house looking for her. When I find Blue Belle she is lying listlessly on her chaise lounge, the big window darkened. I step closer.

"Are you okay?" I ask. She looks at me for a moment through half closed eyes and then slowly shakes her head with an almost imperceptible motion. I step closer.

"Are you sick?" ask, noticing that her arms and delicate face seemed thin for some reason. At this, her eyes open wider and she gives me one long, piercing look and then her lids close completely.

"Go away," she mutters. "You don't love me. You want me to die."

I am struck to the heart. I'm a mother, for God's sake. I want everything to live, even Blue Belle. I move over to the chaise lounge and lean down beside Blue Belle's small figure that suddenly seems so childlike. I raise my hand to touch her, to assure her that I do not want her to die, that she is part of me, that I cannot live without her. But suddenly a hand closes over the wrist of my outstretched arm. The grasp is strong.

I can't move my arm. I look up. Into Bitch's accusing black eyes. For a long moment my heart seems to stop. I want to yell at Bitch to let go of me, to tell her in no uncertain terms that Blue Belle is my business and my business alone. But the words won't come out. Bitch's grip on my wrist tightens. I desperately want Blue Belle to move, or to say something, anything, to break Bitch's spell, to keep me from falling into those blazing unfathomable black eyes that I already know will lead to pain, to awful turbulence, to unremitting anxiety and fear of being ostracized in my later years because I know I will swim against the waters again, my God, I've already been there, done that, and I know it promises nothing in return for such enormous sacrifices.

But Bitch doesn't lessen her grip and Blue Belle doesn't move or speak. I have to make my decision. Now. And I do. I abdicate. I close my eyes against Bitch's unrelenting gaze. Then she lets my arm drop. She knows that she has won, that I will offer no further resistance. I have let Blue Belle go. No longer will I cling to all those wonderful childhood experiences she represents, and later, as a very young mother, the lovely feelings of belonging, of half believing, of trying desperately to believe. I slowly straighten and turn to face Bitch, to turn away from Blue Belle.

"Don't come back in here again," Bitch says in a soft but firm voice. "It's bad for you. Do you agree?"

I nod and stumble out of Blue Belle's quarters, feeling sick. Back in my own rooms I put away all the gospel music. I am finished with it forever, I promise the walls of my tiny little second bedroom. There is a sofa bed in this room, and a large desk that holds my assortments of personal items. The walls are painted blue, a beautiful blue with green undertones. Like sea water. Maybe like the tears blinding my own eyes as I fumble around the top of my desk searching for a box of tissues.

There in the middle of a muddle of papers, I find an empty box, no tissues. But I don't care, I really am finished with Blue Belle forever, I repeat, fiercely wiping my cheeks with the back of my hand. With all she represents. With all the music, the prayers, the preaching, the singing on the grounds, Wednesday night prayer meetings, Sunday School, the church picnics, but most of all the wonderful, beautiful, everlasting singing, my mother playing hymns on the old piano, on the accordion, my sister and brother on the guitar...I can hear them playing and singing still. But I close my ears, wipe my face, sit down to my computer and start writing frantically, pushing Blue Belle from my consciousness.

HURRICANE SANDY, RAPE, and GOD'S WILL?

While the eastern part of Canada and the U.S. await the ravages of Hurricane Sandy we are reminded that what affects the people in these regions affects us all. We are all connected as everything is connected, Global Warming, Climate Change, Politics and Religion.

I was raised in the very bosom of Christian evangelical fundamentalism. I know that the current vicious weather patterns of Climate Change will be regarded as "God's Will" by this very large group that is increasingly trying to take over the US and Canada. They believe that whatever happens is "God's will." However, before a live audience last Tuesday, Indiana Republican for US Senate, Richard Mourdock said something so bizarre that even I was taken aback. He said: "Life is that gift from God. And I think when life begins in that horrible situation of rape that it is something God intended to happen."

And Mourdock has not retracted this statement. Nor has Mitt Romney, US presidential candidate, disowned him. This puts both Mitt Romney and Richard Mourdock on the same intellectual level as their Republican Senate candidate from Missouri Todd Akin, who believes that women can automatically shut down sperm from entering their fallopian tubes when raped if they didn't really want to be raped, that is, if their rape was "legitimate." But I find Richard Mourdock's attempted explanation the day after the debate the most revealing. What exactly did Mourdock say at his press conference the following day in his attempt to explain his position more fully?

He said, and I quote: "I abhor rape. Certainly I did not intend to suggest that God wants rape, that God pushes people to rape."

No? Fundamentalist Christians are usually well versed in the Old Testament of the Bible. The book of Numbers recounts how Moses, after defeating the city of Midian, instructed his commanders:

"So kill all the male children. Kill also all the women who have slept with a man. Spare the lives only of the young girls who have not slept with a man and keep them for yourselves." (Numbers 31:17-18)

And where did Moses get his instructions? Read on: "Moses and Eleazar the priest did as <u>YAHWEH</u> had ordered Moses." (Numbers 31:31-35) And who is Yahweh of the Old Testament? God, that's who.

The Old Testament's stories of the rape of women and little girls (and there are others, equally as shocking) are part and parcel of Christian and Jewish tradition of recognizing the laws of the Old Testament, laws that are also recognized by other patriarchal religions. My thesis is that this Biblical background is exactly where fundamentalist men take their cues on women and climate. The earth, like women, is to be controlled; nature bent to men's will. If the earth and all life on it suffer and even disappears, it doesn't matter, this is "God's will."

And need I remind anybody that our prime minister is also an evangelical fundamentalist Christian? And so are many in his cabinet? And that Prime Minister Harper intends to sneak around his promise not to open the abortion debate by letting his ministers do it? Will anybody be surprised when the abortion issue winds up in the Supreme Court of Canada? And guess who will be waiting there for the issue to appear? Why, the right wing judges that Harper has appointed which will give them the majority on the bench. And guess how the right wing judges will vote? They will vote in "God's will."

Extreme weather patterns are the result of collective decisions made by the banks, corporations, militaries, the oil and gas industry and university and government "sellouts." When fundamentalist religions bless these crimes and deem them "God's will" they seek to numb us and dumb us down to accept any imaginable atrocity brought about by the sexist, racist and economic thievery actions of men who have lied, cheated, and bribed their way into power. Women everywhere are in the most severe jeopardy from these men (and their female clones). We must resist and find the strength to weather the storms. For our children's sake. And we will.

And then I sleep, exhausted. The following morning the rain has socked in.

CHAPTER EIGHTEEN
A Christian burial and
Psychic Androgyny

IN THE KITCHEN I PLUG IN MY LITTLE TWO CUP COFFEE POT while I search the radio stations for news. I find CBC as always. Even though I no longer trust CBC for truthful political news as they just primarily repeat what comes out of Ottawa or Washington, I do trust them more or less, to tell the truth about the weather. Without ads. And it seems New York and New Jersey are being flooded by Hurricane Sandy. The storm appears to be monstrous, threatening huge areas of the American east coast. There are also expectations that Hurricane Sandy will move into Canada around the Great Lakes and also over into Quebec. It's depressing.

And I can't find the cream for my coffee. I must have used it up. I shuffle things around in the fridge. There's milk, but I don't like cooling my coffee down by pouring a lot of cold milk into the cup to get to the desired creamy colour. There isn't any powdered milk, either. Both Marian and Margaret are good about keeping the basic kitchen necessities on hand, I'll have to relearn. In the meantime I'll have to do with the artificial coffee whitener that I impulsively picked up for emergencies when shopping on my own. My daughters reacted with horror when they accidentally discovered the jar. I don't care. I had to drink the artificial whitener in prison. It's all they serve in prison for coffee. If it was a deadly poison as my daughters claim I'd be dead already. And besides, this is an emergency. I am still standing at the sink sipping my truly hot coffee when Bitch appears at the kitchen door.

"It's not good," I announce. "Some deaths and a whole lot of water. There's extensive flooding..."

"I know," Bitch answers slowly. Her voice is heavy, her face shadowed. There is a long silence. I know she has come to tell me something that couldn't wait. It has to be about Blue Belle. I wait, filled with apprehension.

"There is something else," she adds after a moment. "Blue Belle died last night. In her sleep."

I feel a knife slice into my body. Into my stomach? Or is it my heart?

"No..." I whisper.

"Yes. And you need to understand that I have to go, too."

I stare at her, Hurricane Sandy momentarily washed out of my mind.

"Go? What are you talking about..."

"I'll tell you later."

She turns, vanishes. I stand there, dazed by the news of Blue Belle's death on top of the horrific news of Hurricane Sandy. And what did Bitch mean, she had to go, too?

Nothing is making any sense. I decide to take a walk, never mind the rain. My head needs clearing. I find my raincoat with the hood and go outside. My condo building fronts a dead end road and it isn't far to the end of the cul-de-sac. There is a public space between the end of the cul-de-sac and a busy highway. It's a nice green space with some trees and a couple of benches. By the time I get there the rain has turned to a drizzle. I sit down on a wet bench and try to soothe my mind.

After a few minutes, just as I'm beginning to worry that she might not appear, I find Bitch sitting beside me on the bench. She sits wordlessly, staring out into the drizzling mists. I turn to her, waiting for her to speak. She is untouched by the rain. I notice she is wearing her favorite blue jeans with a black sequined top. Is that one of the thrift store tops I bought years ago and never wore? Her feet are bare.

"So...why did you say what you said in the kitchen?" I ask finally, breaking the silence. "That you have to go? What does that mean?"

Bitch turns, facing me. Under the mists, the colour of her eyes is strikingly different. Her eyes aren't dark unto black as usual, but blue-green and crystal clear, like the deep parts of the ocean. Her deep set eyes are so strange and unfamiliar that I quickly look away. She is freaking me out.

"You don't need me anymore," she says slowly. "I was just hanging round until you could get up the guts to let Blue Belle go."

I turn back to her. "I don't understand..." I begin.

She half turns on the bench, compelling me to look at her.

"Do you remember when you were studying the works of Karl Marx and Friedrich Engels, how Engels described the theory of Dialectical materialism?" she asks.

"Vaguely," I answer uncertainly, searching my memory. But what do you and Blue Belle have to do with that..."

"Everything. Remember the discussions around evolution, about how new things come to be because they grow out of their own particular histories and how everything carries within it the seeds of its own destruction..."

"Yes, I do remember," I answer, recalling. "I remember very well. That's the theory of Dialectical materialism. It says that first there is a thesis, which is a thing, or a condition, but after a period of time a certain opposition begins to grow within the thesis and this is called the antithesis. At some point the antithesis becomes as strong as the original thesis and then there is such a conflict that the antithesis can't be held back any longer, and it busts out and becomes something new. This new thing is called the synthesis."

"Good. You do remember. But keep in mind that the synthesis still retains something of the original thesis along with the antithesis within its DNA, so to speak. Like the birth of a baby, remember?"

"I do. I remember those discussions in the group. About how a human baby is kind of a good example of Dialectical materialism The mother is the thesis, the fetus is the antithesis growing inside the womb until it becomes so developed it has to be its own new thing so it demands to be born. But the new baby, who is the synthesis, carriers the history of its parents, both mother and father, within its DNA."

"That's right," Bitch says, her voice warm with approval. "And I would like you to keep this principle in mind in the future. This intellectual construct is important because it will prepare you and other women to face what's ahead with a degree of equanimity. The emotional and intellectual power of the female combined with the female's hatred of violence is gathering strength and will soon, relatively speaking, grip the world. This power has been growing in the womb of history for five thousand years and the labour pains of female revolution have started. Everything is trying to stop the parturition, even women themselves, but it's no use. A new thing knows when it is ready to be born."

I am silent, trying to digest what Bitch is telling me. Is she as serious as all this? Is her off the wall sounding prophecy a serious possibility, that of a coming women's revolution? It just sounds so crazy. And to place so much emphasis on Marx's philosophy when there are all those stories about how he fathered an illegitimate child, a son, by Helene Demuth, the family's servant. That has always irked me, the image of Marx sneaking around in the middle of the night and hopping into his servant's bed. But Bitch reads my mind.

"Those stories may or may not be true," she says, breaking into my thoughts.

"The father of Helene Demuth's son may have been Friedrich Engels. For our purposes it doesn't matter. All human thought is tainted by the oppression of women but it's the only thought we've got to work with at the moment. And using Dialectical materialism to help us think about the world can be useful. We can see evolution all around us, in children, in plants, animals, in the way that Mother Nature is responding to the enormous threats of global warming."

"But there's Blue Belle," I offer after a moment. I don't understand..."

"Yes, you do. On some level, anyway. Think. In your historical past, Blue Belle was the thesis. She actually existed centuries before you came on the scene, at least for the last five thousand years. During that time men overthrew the power and influence of women, and the new religious ideas and inspirations that exploded on the scene came from men who desired above all, to control women. Blue Belle was simply the thesis you knew and could identify with because she was there when you were born and you grew up with her. I'm the antithesis to Blue Belle. I exist for you only in relation to Blue Belle. I came because you invited me, because something in you called out to me, vaguely at first, and undecided, but then your invitation became louder and stronger with time because you wanted to know. And because you asked for help I came. I came as the antithesis to Blue Belle. But I exist only in relation to Blue Belle. She is dead now, so there is no reason for me to stay."

"No, I don't want you to go," I protest. "You will leave me unprotected..."

"You are not unprotected. You understand more than you think you do. You, in a sense, are the synthesis that Marx and Engels spoke about. By reaching for more justice, more equality, more love in the world, you are asking for a new society. And your expanding consciousness is also reaching out toward the psychic androgyny that Mary Daly described. Androgyny combines characteristics of both male and female into one being, right?"

"No, I'm not ready for this,' I wail, swiping back the dripping wet bangs plastered to my forehead.

"Yes, you are. You know how to find the books and papers you need to write authoritatively. But find a new copy of Evelyn Reed's Evolution of Women. Your old one is torn to shreds. And stop eating peanut butter and jelly sandwiches when you read. I hated looking at your materials with bits of jelly and jam smeared here and there. It's unprofessional."

I give a start. She's accusing me of being unprofessional? Of appearing unprofessional in any way? She, queen of the scarecrows of the underworld?

"And there's great new stuff out," she goes on, evidently oblivious to the contraindications of the little homily she is delivering to me. "Read Iain McGilchrist's book on the human brain, and of course you are already gathering material on maternal Mitochondrial DNA, and you're also on the right track with the Grandmother Hypothesis, and...anyway, I've got to go. I'm taking Blue Belle back to Louisiana this morning for a proper southern burial. There will be lots of preaching and singing and praising the Lord. You just keep your eye on the prize."

She stands up abruptly and turns as if to go. Feeling a surge of panic, I rise searching for words to retain her longer.

"No, wait," I beg, trying to keep panic out of my voice. She pauses, facing me again, her expression slightly irritated.

"What is the prize?" I demand.

"I thought you knew," she says impatiently. "The prize is peace. And we'll get it when women rule the world."

Before I can answer, before I can further entreat her to stay, Bitch is gone. And she has made it clear I will never see or hear from her again. Or from Blue Belle. I'm on my own.

The sudden surge of panic I had felt a few moments earlier subsides, but leaves a hollow feeling in the pit of my stomach. On my way home the drizzle becomes a steady downpour. After a hot bath and a cup of hot chocolate I feel a strong urge to call somebody and tell them what has happened, that Blue Belle has died and that Bitch has taken her back to

Louisiana for burial and that I will never see either of them again. But who would I tell?

There is nobody to tell. Blue Belle and Bitch were real only to me. And to Hoffman, Marian's cat. If Harriet Nahanee were alive I would tell her. She would certainly understand. She was delving into the same histories before she died, our human and environmental histories, but from different starting points. Her version of the Stockholm Syndrome helped me focus; helps me still. Harriet is far from the casualties of my inner battlefield and its aftermath, and yet somehow in the centre of it all.

By the time of Longfellow's Children's Hour the rain has stopped. I love the poem and the early evening the time of day it evokes. My mother used to recite Children's Hour to us by heart. As a child I wondered about the three little girls that Longfellow describes in the poem. Oh, how I longed for a father like the one they had! I couldn't understand how Mama could love poetry and literature and Daddy at the same time. Perhaps we will never understand our parents. But I loved my mother dearly and it was the biggest struggle of my life to strike Blue Belle out of my heart and mind because she was so close to my mother. In fact, Blue Belle was in cahoots with Mama.

Aw, yes. Of course it was Blue Belle who kept me anchored to the old memories of home and church, my love of the old gospel music, the Sunday dinners, on the church grounds if the weather was nice, inside the church if it was raining, the huge mounds of fried chicken that had been fried by mothers in the early morning before getting ready for church, before getting the children ready, the large platters of potato salad and coleslaw, baked sweet potatoes, the pans of cornbread and biscuits, the big bowls of banana pudding and tins of pecan pie, and always a berry cobbler that sometimes dripped on the pretty, freshly-starched cotton dresses my mother made that my sister and I wore to church, with our hair in artificial ringlets, tightly curled from the Saturday night hair washing and the painful process of setting with rag curlers, the dimes in our little Sunday School envelopes that we proudly placed in the offering plate when it was passed by the deacons in the main church service and always, at the end of the service the invitation to "come to Jesus and be saved."

Memories of this kind of a childhood are like an iron stake covered in the sweetest pink velvet driven directly into the hearts of innocents. Pulling that stake all the way out can take a lifetime. Certainly it did for me. I am old. I am lucky. Because some people never conclude the business at all and pass out of this world with a half concealed iron stake still buried in their heart.

But the final battle of my own struggle is over. Bitch is right. I don't need her anymore. Or Blue Belle. Now I am free to recognize the evils of the religious system of sexism and racism not only intellectually and politically, but to acknowledge what it is emotionally. "That Old Time Religion," the old foot stomping hymn everybody knew and could belt out lustily was deeply imprinted on my brain:

> Gimme that old time religion,
> that was good for our fathers,
> that was good for our mothers,
> and it's good enough for me.

But it wasn't. And it isn't. However, that old time religion is right now stalking not just an unsophisticated southern US and swaths of Canada, but Latin America, Africa and parts of Europe, too.

And inevitably, wherever that old time religion establishes itself, it plays out its political agenda against women, banning or trying to ban birth control, abortion, and equal rights for women. In the treatment of women that old time Christian religion sits side by side with the Muslim world which seeks, with its strong influences, to get their Old Time Religions going, too, in Sharia Law. These two religious belief systems have tolerated and perpetuated every crime against nature and humanity known to us.

That Old time Christian religion, from the bottom to the top, doesn't seem to believe in cutting off body parts for punishment or stoning women to death. But it works very well with corporations and doesn't seem to mind at all poisoning the body politic with pollution or causing wars or refusing aid to people and countries who don't believe that western style democracy is the best way to go, or that Jesus Christ is their Saviour. But my own decks are cleared. I will work, as long as I am able, to try to convince women to come in out of the cold of patriarchal religions and patriarchal institutions and begin to build a new world where women and children and nature are respected by everybody. When that happens the world will right itself.

But now a monster storm is raging on the east coast of the US; many people are huddling in the dark without light or heat, shivering in water-soaked dwellings, with the temperatures dropping. My heart is with them, as are the hearts and minds of millions of others around the world. At this point nobody knows how destructive Hurricane Sandy will eventually be. Or who will win the American election. All I can do as an individual at this juncture of time is make this promise to Mother Earth...

Mother of us all, wherever I am, whatever I do, I know I am in your hands. My only weapon against the forces threatening to destroy the billions of years of evolution you have provided is mothers' concern for the earth and its inhabitants, especially the young...not only our human children, but also the young of the forests, the seas and the skies, all creatures everywhere...that these mothers' concerns be raised to a fierce passionate rage, but a rage laced with humility. There are many women rising in the world today. Collectively, the passionate rage of women will ready us all for the intense storms we are facing now and into the future. This passionate collective rage will take us through to the next stage of human evolution, men and women alike, of all races that together portend a new human consciousness. Are you okay with this, Harriet Nahanee?

THE END

OTHER BOOKS
BY BETTY KRAWCZYK

Clayoquot The Sound of My Heart	Orca Publishing 1996
Lock Me Up or Let Me Go	1st edition Raincoast Books 2002
	2nd printing Schiver Rhodes Publishing 2011
Open Living Confidential	Schiver Rhodes Publishing 2007
This Dangerous Place	Schiver Rhodes Publishing 2011

CPSIA information can be obtained at www.ICGtesting.com
Printed in the USA
LVOW06s2007190614

390830LV00001B/280/P

9 781460 226292